WHY I AM A PROTESTANT

WHY I AM A PROTESTANT

by

RUPERT E. DAVIES

Tutor in Church History
and the History of Christian Doctrine
at Didsbury College, Bristol

LONDON
THE EPWORTH PRESS

THE EPWORTH PRESS
(FRANK H. CUMBERS)
25-35 City Road, London, E.C.1

MELBOURNE   CAPE TOWN
NEW YORK   TORONTO

SET IN MONOTYPE BASKERVILLE AND PRINTED IN
GREAT BRITAIN BY THE CAMELOT PRESS LTD
LONDON AND SOUTHAMPTON

TO MY DAUGHTER
MARY

CONTENTS

FOREWORD

THIS BOOK is in two parts. In the first I try to set out my reasons for being a Protestant; in the second are my reasons for rejecting Roman Catholicism.

I make here a personal profession of faith, which binds nobody but myself. But it may be that the reasons for which I must be a Protestant and cannot be a Roman Catholic will be of interest to other Protestants who wish to be surer of their faith, and to those people who are attracted by some parts of Roman Catholic doctrine. I even dare to hope that some who have embraced the Roman Catholic faith will read what I have written, with their minds open to truth.

I am a Methodist, a Protestant and a Catholic. I therefore pray that this book may tend, not to further division, but to the greater unity of the Holy Catholic Church, which is the Body of Christ and the People of God.

RUPERT E. DAVIES

DIDSBURY COLLEGE
BRISTOL
October 1956

Part One

THE NATURE OF PROTESTANTISM

CHAPTER ONE

What is a Protestant?

THE WORD 'Protestant' has fallen on evil times. Once it was a highly respectable, very honourable term, so much so that it finds a place in the Coronation Service of the realm of Great Britain. But now there are many within the Church of England who declare that their Church is not Protestant at all, and many others who, although they maintain that their Church is both Catholic and Protestant, rather wish that it had not been saddled with the latter term, and that the more neutral word 'Reformed' had been used instead. In fact, there is a widely held view in Anglicanism, and beyond in the wider circles of the Ecumenical Movement in England, that the only Protestants left are those who are militantly and aggressively Protestant, to the extent of forming leagues and societies for the purpose of defending the existence of Protestantism and asserting Protestant principles in the teeth of their opponents.

This denigration of the term 'Protestant' springs partly from the success of the Oxford Movement in persuading Anglicans that their Church is the 'Catholic Church of this island' (though both Roman Catholics and Free Churchmen, for very different reasons, would deny the claim), and that the Protestant Reformers of the Church of England really interrupted the course of its true history; but it springs much more from a sheer misunderstanding of the meaning of the word, both by its friends and by its enemies, and of the function which the Protestant Churches essay to perform within the One, Holy, Catholic Church, under the rule of the Lord of the Church and the guidance of the Holy Spirit.

Most people's idea of a Protestant nowadays is of a man who makes it his main business to protest against abuses, of a man with a negative outlook, who looks sourly at the achievements of other Churches, and is always on the watch to object to the most innocent practices on the part of those with whom he disagrees and to label them as Romish and superstitious. This conception has been fostered to some extent by the deservedly popular writings of that group of writers who have gone over from a merely nominal Protestantism to a genuine Catholicism, and now, like all converts, take a jaundiced view of that from which they have been converted; they identify in their minds the restrictive religious practices in which their parents vainly tried to bring them up with the essence of Protestantism. No one can doubt that they have some excuse for so doing in the caricature of Protestantism, angular, unctuous, and Philistine, which did duty for the real thing in some Nonconformist and Low Church households not so very long ago.

It is time, clearly, to reinstate the true meaning of the word. Its historical origin is of very great importance and determines its basic sense, though it does not, of course, control all the shades of meaning which it has subsequently acquired. In the year 1526, not long after Germany and much of the rest of Europe had been plunged into a great religious upheaval by the teachings and acts of Martin Luther, the Diet, that is, the supreme council, of the Holy Roman Empire met in the city of Speier. There was a long and fruitless discussion between the opponents and the supporters of reform, and there was seen to be no chance of agreement. Meanwhile the Turks were advancing into Europe, and the whole Empire was in peril. Unity was necessary at almost any cost, and the princes who favoured the retention of the old religion finally accepted a compromise by which each ruler was to determine the religion, reformed or unreformed, of his own country. He was 'so to live, govern, and carry himself as he hopes and trusts to answer it to God and His Imperial Majesty'. Thus the reformed religion was tolerated throughout the Empire in those countries where the ruling prince so decreed. One of the reasons which induced the Emperor to agree to this was the fact that he was on bad terms with the Pope.

During the next three years the menace from the East receded, and the Emperor and the Pope were reconciled. In 1529 the Diet met again at Speier. The supporters of the 'old religion' were in a considerable majority, and carried a decree which effectually revoked the decision of the previous Diet of Speier. It enacted that those who denied the Roman doctrine of the Mass should not be tolerated by the Empire or allowed to preach in public. The earlier decision had been unanimous; this one was carried against the votes of six princes and fourteen cities of the Empire. The minority thereupon drew up a document to present to the Emperor, which they called a 'Protestation'. This document does indeed protest *against* the way in which the reforming princes had been treated by the Diet, and in particular against the setting aside of a unanimous vote by that of a majority; but its main purpose is a positive one, that of 'protesting' the Christian faith as these princes and cities understood it. The word 'Protestant' came into currency from the document which the members of the Speier minority promulgated; and it means primarily someone who protests his faith according to the teaching of the evangelical reformers, or, as the reformers themselves would have said, according to the teaching of the Word of God. Thus the word denotes a 'protester of his faith', an affirmer, proclaimer of his faith.

Of course, in the circumstances of the time, there were many things in the life of the Church against which the Protestants felt themselves in conscience bound to protest, and did most vehemently protest, and that has often been true also in the succeeding centuries. Thus the word comes to connote an 'objector to abuses'. But this is a secondary sense, and for a Catholic or a Protestant to put the secondary sense in the place of the primary sense is to misconceive the whole nature of the religious convictions which lay behind the Reformation and which lie behind the specific witness of Protestants today.

A Protestant, then, is primarily one who proclaims the Christian Faith. But the title involves something else as well. Those who have applied it to themselves have, as a matter of history, always claimed that the Bible is the sole source of the Christian Faith as they proclaim it. How far this claim is justified will be seen later; we are concerned for the moment only with the important fact that the Protestant claims that his is a biblical Christianity, whatever anyone else's Christianity may be. Protestants have held different views at different times about the exact authority to be ascribed to the words of the Bible; there have been periods—not including, be it said, the first age of the Reformation—when they have regarded every word and sentence in it as equally authoritative and in every case infallible, and there are some Protestants who hold this view today. But belief in the inerrancy of Scripture does not belong to the essence of Protestantism, and most of its leaders no longer hold it. What does belong to the essence of Protestantism, at every moment of its history, is the conviction that the Bible is for the Christian the sole and sufficient repository of truth, that every doctrine must be brought to the touchstone of the Bible, and that any theology worthy of the name 'Christian' must be a biblical theology.

Under the heading of Protestant, thus defined by original meaning and history, come the Lutheran Churches of Germany, Scandinavia, and America; the Reformed, or Presbyterian, Churches of Switzerland, Holland, Germany, Scotland, and all other parts of the English-speaking world; the Congregational, Baptist, and Methodist Churches spread over the world; a number of smaller Churches which have branched off from the great Protestant Churches; and many members of the Anglican communion.

CHAPTER TWO

Protestants and the Bible

IT WILL be seen at once that the Protestant reliance on the Bible as the sole source of Christian doctrine necessary for salvation has certain disadvantages. The early Reformers believed that the meaning of the Bible was perfectly plain to anyone who read it with faith in his heart; and that if any difficulty arose it could be easily resolved by comparing one part of the Bible with another. This was the reason behind their advocacy of the 'open Bible'. If everyone is allowed and encouraged to read the Bible in his own language, they thought, he will quickly gain the sense of it (a sense which would, of course, be almost exactly the same sense as that gained and taught by the Reformers themselves), the strongholds of error and superstition will be rapidly overthrown, and the whole Church will be once again founded on the one truth. But we know better. The Bible is not so easy as all that to understand. The ordinary believer very often does not understand it at all, and when he thinks he understands it, he often gets the meaning wrong. And what the scholars gave as the meaning of many passages in the sixteenth century is very often entirely rejected by the scholars of today.

But the worst thing of all is that good men, honest men, Christian men, learned men, have often disagreed, and still do disagree, about the meaning of many central passages in the Bible. All Roman Catholics are quite certain that Jesus appointed St Peter and his successors as the Head of the Church, on the basis of Matthew 16[18]: 'Thou art Peter, and upon this rock I will build my church.' Protestants are equally certain that the passage can bear no such meaning. And similar differences occur within Protestantism. Protestants of the Baptist tradition are convinced that the Baptism of infants is completely inconsistent with the whole tenor of New Testament teaching; other Protestants are convinced that it expresses New Testament teaching. Examples of this could, of course, be multiplied indefinitely.

Here we come up against the real stumbling-block of Protestantism. The different possible ways of interpreting the Scriptures furnish the principal cause of that 'proliferation of sects' with which Catholics are prone to taunt the Protestant world. From differing views about the New Testament's descriptions of Church Order come the differing principles of episcopalianism, congregationalism, and presbyterianism; from divergent interpretations of the Epistle to the Romans come predestination and Arminianism; from varying explanations of the passages describing the Second Coming come the multicoloured apocalyptic sects of our own and earlier times; from diverse conceptions of the work of the Holy Spirit, all derived from the New Testament, come the Methodists, the Quakers, and the Pentecostalists—and so on.

The Catholic way of preventing all this is well known. Let the Church, to whom Jesus promised that the Holy Spirit would lead it into all the truth, formulate and promulgate the true meaning of the Scriptures, not once and for all, for there are doctrines hidden in the Scriptures which the Church is authorized to disclose one by one to succeeding generations, but steadily and gradually; yet in the case of each successive pronouncement, definitively and finally. Then all the faithful, instructed or uninstructed, will know what the Bible really means, and be preserved from the temptation of wandering down the paths of error at the impulse of this or that private insight or current theory. Thus the unity of the Church will be maintained and the doctrines of Scripture unanimously proclaimed.

Later in this book this doctrine of the infallibility of the Church will be discussed. Here it may be pointed out that the doctrine has not, in point of historical fact, had the desired effect. It is a mistake to think that the

Church was undivided and indivisible until the Reformers carried through a policy of fragmentation. The strict formulation of doctrine by an authoritative Church has never prevented either heresy or schism; in some cases it has encouraged them. Arianism not only asserted itself against the Council of Nicaea in A.D. 325; it maintained itself for many centuries against the Council of Constantinople of A.D. 381. Nestorianism still exists, at least officially, in several of the Churches of the East, in spite of the Council of Ephesus in A.D. 431. The views of Eutyches were condemned by the Council of Chalcedon in A.D. 451; but the Church in Egypt and several other countries never accepted its decisions, and remained in complete separation. The great Orthodox Churches of Eastern Christendom have been out of communion with Rome for more than eight hundred years, and show no signs of returning to it. So much for heresy. Cases of long-continued schism on grounds of order or discipline from the one, authoritative Church—Montanism, Novatianism, Donatism, Priscillianism, Waldensianism, and the rest—have been even more numerous. It does not seem from these examples that even an infallible Church prevents the Bible from being variously interpreted—if the Reformation itself did not provide incontestable proof of that by itself alone.

Yet the fissiparousness of Protestantism must be acknowledged, and acknowledged as a scandal. Is it too high a price to pay for the examination of the Bible as the sole source of Christian doctrine? Not, surely, if this view of the Bible is true to the facts; still less, if there is some hope of removing the scandal. And no Protestant doubts that both these conditions are fulfilled.

Be it noted that the Protestant claim, except in certain circles whose authoritarianism resembles that of Rome, is not that the Bible is infallible. Only Jesus Christ, the Word of God, is infallible. In Him—the only-begotten Son of God, born of Mary, who lived, taught, and worked in Palestine in the first century A.D., was crucified, rose again, ascended to the Father, and will come again to judge the living and the dead—is all we know, and all we need to know, for the salvation of our souls. This is a far more fundamental conviction for Protestants than anything that we say about the authority of the Bible. In this sense it is not true to say, with Chillingworth, that 'the Bible and the Bible only is the religion of Protestants'. Our faith, our ultimate, total faith, is not in what the Bible, or any book or document or personage, says, but in Christ and in Christ alone; it is not an acceptance of any propositions, however venerable, however soundly vouched-for by Council or Pope or sacred book, but a personal trust in a Person, in the only Person who deserves or can receive such trust, Jesus Christ our Lord.

Of the truth as it is in Christ no human record is guaranteed free from error. This may seem a hard saying even to some Protestants. If we do not know for certain, beyond a peradventure, what Christ did and said, are we not still floundering in darkness and ignorance? Has our religion not failed to give us the very thing, certain knowledge of the ultimate meaning of life, by the promise of which it persuaded us to embrace it? It has to be said—and for many people this is a hard, unpalatable truth, which they seek to evade by taking refuge in one or other of the systems, all differing from each other, which are falsely labelled 'infallible'—that to ask for this kind of certainty is to cry for the moon. It is not granted to us, or to any man, in this life. If it were, why should it be granted to some and not to others? And if it were granted to some and not to others, how should we know, with our own fallible minds, who they were to whom it was granted? In this life, we live by faith and not by sight; in the next, we shall know even as we are already known.

But the Bible is our primary, and all-important, witness to Christ, to His words, His deeds, His sufferings, His resurrection and ascension, and to the teaching which those who had known Him personally in the flesh, and had learned from His own lips, gave to the world and to those whom they gathered out of the world. No other source of information enters, or can enter, into the most distant comparison with the Bible in this matter. The Bible stands alone, unchallenged. This is a matter of plain, historical fact, ascertainable and ascertained by all the means available to students of the past, and therefore scientifically verifiable in a way in which the truths of theology, by the very nature of the case, can never be verified. We are not saying, of course, that every word in the New Testament is scientifically verifiable; we are saying that to read the New Testament is necessarily superior to any other possible way of finding out the truth about Christ, and that if the New Testament were removed we should have no reliable way of knowing about Christ at all. In actual fact, it is also true that scientific investigation of what the New Testament says about Christ reveals a remarkable historical accuracy, but that is another, though very important, matter.

Therefore we cannot do otherwise than regard the Bible as the sole source of Christian doctrine necessary for salvation. There are other truths which it is valuable to know which are not to be found in Holy Scripture. These relate to the many departments of human knowledge on which the Bible does not pretend to be an authority—science, art, poetry, economics, large areas of human history, and so forth. Some relate to theology, on which the Bible does claim to be an authority. Truths of the former type are left open by the Bible and Protestantism for free investigation and inquiry. Truths of the latter type can hardly be necessary for salvation, for men and women were saved before they were revealed, but they may be valuable additions to our knowledge of God and man; they need, of course, to be tested by the touchstone of Scripture. Sometimes we can bring the two types of 'supplementary' truth together by showing that advance in knowledge of science has widened and deepened our knowledge of God; this is especially true of the doctrine of creation. But these considerations do not affect the Protestant doctrine of the sufficiency of the Bible as the source of necessary Christian knowledge.

B

We have seen something of the cost of this doctrine to the Church in division and disagreement. But it may be that the time is coming when this cost will have been paid, or almost paid, in full. The Reformation gave an impetus, completely unknown before, to the study of the Scriptures. Naturally enough, this study led to divisions of opinion which have often seemed endless, and endlessly ramified. But this period of divisiveness shows signs of drawing to an end, at least as far as the main teachings of the Bible are concerned. Scholars of all denominations, except, alas, for the most part those of the Roman Church, are becoming more and more agreed about the theology of the Bible, Old and New Testament alike; and the differences that remain, some of them still deep, frequently cut across denominational frontiers. It is not at all unusual to find Baptists and Anglicans joining hands on some point of biblical theology against other Baptists and other Anglicans. Most significantly of all, there is coming to be very general agreement among scholars of all schools of thought and all denominational affiliations about the framework and content of the teaching of Jesus, about the teaching of the apostles concerning Jesus, and even, though many people still find this incredible, about the New Testament doctrine of the Church.

Without this growth into unity on the teaching of the Bible, the Ecumenical Movement would have been impossible. Or perhaps it would be truer to say that this unity is one of the surest foundations of the Ecumenical Movement. Time and again it has been possible to point out, within that Movement, that the historical cleavages which have resulted from conflicting interpretations of certain passages in the Bible are now at an end, and that therefore progress is possible which would have been inconceivable to our forefathers. These facts give great hope that the doctrine of the sufficiency of Scripture will lead in the future not to diversity but to unity, or, better still, to unity in diversity.

CHAPTER THREE

What Protestants Believe

IT SOMETIMES comes as a surprise to Catholics, of all kinds, to find how much we believe of what they believe. Having been taught that schism always leads to the corruption and watering-down of the faith, they at once suppose that Protestants, whom they believe to be in a state of schism, have corrupted and watered-down the faith. We have certainly, on occasion, given ample excuse for such an opinion. We have sometimes seemed to reject a doctrine just because it was held by the Roman Church—only to find out later that the doctrine was not so foolish after all. The Roman Church holds, for instance, that the efficacy of the Sacraments is not at all affected by the personal character of the officiating minister, since the Sacrament is the gift of God and not of man; Protestants have leaped in the past to the other extreme of supposing that a Sacrament was only valid if it was administered by a minister who was truly worthy. But most of us now would acknowledge the strength of the Roman contention, at least in a modified form. Then there was a period at the end of the last century and the beginning of this, when, largely under the influence of political liberalism and individualistic tendencies in most departments of thought, many Protestant thinkers sat loose to the dogmas of orthodoxy; and this episode in the history of Protestantism has been taken, not unnaturally, but falsely, to be typical of Protestantism in itself. Some Protestants, too, are unwilling that the Creeds of the Church should be said in public worship, in case there should be any present who could not wholeheartedly assent to all the clauses—and it is true that the Protestant Churches for the most part do not demand

exact adherence to the Creeds as a condition of membership. This has been taken to mean that the Creeds are
not believed among the Protestants in question, though
in fact this is not so at all.

It is necessary, therefore, to state quite unequivocally
that the Protestant Churches, as defined at the end of
Chapter 1, accept the Apostles' Creed, the Creed of
Nicaea, the Creed of Constantinople (commonly called
the 'Nicene Creed'), and the Creed of Chalcedon, as true
statements of the Christian Faith. It has to be added
that Churches of the Congregationalist and Baptist traditions reserve to each congregation the right to state its
own faith in such terms as it may choose for itself, but
there is no reason to think that many such congregations
would refuse their assent to these Creeds, even if they
did not formally adopt them. Protestantism does not
thereby place the historic Creeds of the Church above,
or on the same level as, the Scriptures. It accepts the
Creeds, and perhaps the Nicene Creed in particular, as
embodying in accurate form the faith of the Bible, and
as convenient summaries, therefore, of biblical theology.

The clauses in the Creeds concerning the Holy Catholic
Church and the Sacrament of Baptism are discussed in
later chapters. Here two comments may be made on
other parts of the Creeds. The first concerns the Person
of Christ. It is customary in Protestant Churches to lay
rather greater stress on the Perfect Humanity of Jesus
Christ than is general in the Churches of the various
Catholic traditions; this custom has its dangers, such as
the possibility of reducing Jesus to a purely human figure,
as was sometimes done by those who were more concerned with the Jesus of history than with the Saviour
of the world. But the opposite danger is observable in
the Catholic traditions, in some of which the human
Jesus has virtually disappeared from the devotion, public
and private, of Christian people. There is no excuse for
this in the Nicene Creed or in the Chalcedonian Definition; yet it has happened many times. Even St Thomas
Aquinas finds it very difficult to ascribe to Jesus any

human virtues. Martin Luther, above all men, brought the Church back to the human life and nature of Jesus. Thus on the central doctrine of the faith, the Incarnation, Protestantism is often more orthodox than Rome—though not, of course, Protestantism in all its periods of history and in all its forms.

The other comment concerns the Holy Spirit. The Creeds are not at all explicit about Him. In fact, it is only the Nicene Creed which does more than mention Him. Protestantism has a very full and rich experience of the Holy Spirit, and, at its best, a full and rich doctrine of the Holy Spirit. This is understandable enough, for in a sense it owes everything to Him. He called it into existence, and has sustained it all through the stormy centuries since the Reformation; therefore it must salute Him as in every sense the Lord and Life-Giver, and go on to claim for Him that He moulds the life of the Church according to the will of God and sanctifies men and women according to the pattern of Jesus Christ. Thus the Protestant Churches have a more satisfying, and more completely orthodox, doctrine of the Holy Spirit than the Creeds enunciate or the Roman Church teaches.

There is one great doctrine of the New Testament and, therefore, of Protestants, to which the Creeds make no reference at all, and that is the doctrine of Justification by Grace. The omission may be simply due to the fact that no controversy on the subject had arisen when the creeds were written, and therefore there was no need to formulate the doctrine. A more likely explanation is that the doctrine itself had been almost submerged in the Church from the time of the New Testament until the time of St Augustine, and was then almost submerged again from the time of St Augustine until the time of the Reformation. It is one of the major tragedies of Christian history that Rome, reminded of the doctrine by Luther and Calvin, nevertheless at the Council of Trent determined so to formulate its doctrine of justification as to exclude once for all from its system all traces of Reformation doctrine on the subject. No doubt Luther and Calvin had reminded Rome of the *sola gratia* in too provocative a fashion; but it is still a thousand pities that Rome, even after long consideration, reacted in the way in which it did.

Luther's crucial objection to the official teachers of his time was that they informed sinful, ignorant people that they could earn the forgiveness of God by the performance of good deeds and faithful acts of devotion, ordinary and extraordinary—alms, masses, pilgrimages, acts of penance and the like. And when the preachers of the Indulgence of 1517 went so far as to say, or plainly to imply, that the mere payment of money to a good cause (and was it a good cause?) would reduce or eliminate the period that souls must spend in Purgatory, the spark was applied which kindled his mind to fiery zeal in the proclamation of the Gospel of sheer grace. Now it is true that the popular teachers of the time were not rightly construing the official doctrine of the Church. It is also true, and even more important, that St Thomas Aquinas had propounded a doctrine of grace which was not wholly inconsistent with Luther's own doctrine. For though he had said that man cannot be accepted by God on the score of his merit, he had added that the merit was given to him by God Himself; though he had said that man must have love to be acceptable to God, he had added that God gives that love to him; though he had said that man must have faith if God is to justify him, he had added that God gives man the faith that He requires of him. Thus he held that there is no salvation without merit; but there is no merit without grace. St Thomas and Luther, if they had met, could have found a formula of agreement. But the fact remains that the teaching of Thomas was not taught, or wholeheartedly accepted, by those who formed the minds of the sixteenth-century Church, and that Luther's charge against its official teachers stands unrefuted.

Luther contended with complete confidence, and Protestants today contend with equal confidence, that according to the New Testament a man is forgiven solely and completely by the grace of God, without any human merit whatsoever; that grace is the undeserved, freely moving favour of God toward sinners, and that it is accepted by faith in Christ—that is, by personal trust, a trust involving the whole self, in a personal Saviour. Of course, such faith, out of sheer gratitude to God for His goodness to man, immediately issues in good deeds and a different manner of life, and if there is no such issue there is no faith present after all. But the good deeds and the changed life do, and can do, nothing whatever to deserve, invite, or invoke the forgiveness of God.

It cannot, unfortunately, be maintained that Protestants have always, or even more often than not, lived up to this high doctrine of the grace of God; there is a down-dragging tendency in every man, and in every religion, which makes it much easier and more gratifying to believe that good deeds and characters in some small way entitle a man to God's favourable consideration. But salvation by grace through faith is the inalienable heritage of Protestantism, the truth which has above all been committed to it to preserve for the whole Church.

CHAPTER FOUR

Protestants and the Church

'THERE IS no other means of entering into life unless the Church conceive us in the womb and give us birth, unless she nourish us at her breasts, and, in short, keeps us under her charge and government, until, divested of mortal flesh, we become like the angels. For our weakness does not permit us to leave the school until we have spent our whole lives as scholars. Moreover, beyond the pale of the Church no forgiveness of sins, no salvation, can be hoped for. . . . The paternal favour of God and the special evidence of spiritual life are confined to his peculiar people, and hence the abandonment of the Church is always fatal.' These are the words of John Calvin, and they express the Protestant doctrine of the Church as it would be accepted by Luther, Zwingli, and all the great Protestant Reformers. It is still the Protestant doctrine.

We hold, in fact, that a man cannot be a Christian without being a member of the Church of Christ, for the Bible, as John Wesley was never tired of asserting, 'knows nothing of a solitary Christian'; in the New Testament, a Christian, by the very fact that he is a Christian, is a member of the Church, the People of God and the Body of Christ. The same act of faith which joins a man to Christ places him in the Church of Christ; he cannot belong to Christ without belonging to His Body; he cannot obey the Kingly Rule of God without becoming a member of His covenanted People. The attitude of the man who says 'I am a Christian, but I have no use for the Church' is inconceivable in the New Testament. It exists, of course, in the modern world, is often perfectly sincere, and is sometimes, very plainly, the result of the failure of the Churches to embody the spirit of Christ.

It means that a man who belongs to Christ, and by that fact to the Church, never takes up his membership or appropriates the blessings which are his, just as many citizens of the British Commonwealth never take up their citizenship by exercising their votes. But such a man is still a member of the Body of Christ.

Calvin, in the words just quoted, is speaking of the visible Church of Christ, the Church on earth as it actually exists, with a history, a ministry and a structure, with sacraments and organization, with buildings and bank accounts, with a list of members and a place in the life of society. It is to this Church that we are attached, not to some vague spiritual fellowship of believers. To this Church, as Calvin makes abundantly plain in his exhaustive treatment of the subject, we are to give our loyal and practical obedience, by attending its services, by concerning ourselves with the details of its life, by accepting office within it if we are called thereto, and by dropping our contribution into the collection-box when it is placed before us. It was to the reform of this Church according to the Word of God that Luther and Calvin addressed every atom of their ability and strength; it was in zeal for the purity of this Church that the English Independents and Baptists felt themselves forced to break away from the Established Church, because it was Established and therefore impure, and to mould afresh the structure of the Church of God in this country and beyond the seas; it was to revive the mission of this Church to spread Scriptural Holiness throughout the world that John and Charles Wesley believed themselves raised up by God.

There is, of course, a difference of opinion between Catholics and Protestants as to where the visible Church is to be found, and what are its marks. We shall discuss the Roman view in the second part of this book. Anglo-Catholics hold that the Church is present wherever the succession of Bishops by the laying-on of hands from the Apostles is preserved. The Protestant view is sharply distinguished from all forms of the Catholic view, all of which require the historic succession of Bishops for the existence of the Church. Luther recognized the presence of the Church by the Sacraments of Baptism and the Eucharist and by the preaching of the Gospel, or, in his later years, by seven marks: the preaching of the Word, the Holy Sacrament of Baptism, the Holy Sacrament of the Altar, the Keys of Christian Discipline and Forgiveness, a called and consecrated Christian Ministry, Public Thanksgiving to and Worship of God, and Christian Suffering. Calvin simplified this by saying that the Church of Christ is present wherever the Gospel is truly preached and the Sacraments duly administered. Perhaps we can put the view that would be accepted by the vast majority of Protestants today by saying that wherever the Gospel is faithfully preached, the Sacraments of the Gospel duly administered, and the Christian life faithfully lived, there is the Church. This is how we understand the words of St Ignatius of Antioch at the beginning of the second century A.D.: 'Where Christ is, there is the Church'; and we refuse to tie down the operation of the Holy Spirit in the Church to a particular form of Church Order, or a particular way of preserving the continuity of Christian truth, life and witness. So, in the words of the Methodist Catechism of 1952: 'Wherever Christ is, there is the Church, and His presence is shown by the preaching of the Word, the administration of the Sacraments, and the living of the Christian life.' It is in this sense that the Church is 'the congregation of all Christ's faithful people'.

It is worth noticing that the Reformation doctrine of the Church never unchurched the Church of Rome. Luther says: 'The Roman Church is holy, because it has the Holy Name of God, Baptism and the Word'; and Calvin, while remarking that the Church of Rome as a whole has not the marks of the true Church, says that many Churches in it have those marks. So today we would say that the Church of Rome is part of the one Church of Christ; it is not the Church, but it is within the Church.

It is generally held that Protestants are more concerned with the invisible Church than with the visible Church. We have seen that this is a misconception, and its removal may well advance the cause of Christian unity, since Catholics of all kinds dislike the idea of the invisible Church and rightly claim that it has no place in Scripture. Nevertheless, Luther and Calvin did speak much, in different ways, of the invisible Church. They were faced with a theological problem which vexes all reformers of the Church. The Church of Rome claimed to be the Church of God; yet it was quite plain that there were leaders and members of it who, by the evidence of their life, were certainly not members of the true Church of Christ. Perhaps the two great Reformers should not have judged other men by such evidence, or at all; but who would now claim that every Pope, Cardinal, Bishop, priest and layman who professed membership of the Church in the sixteenth century was truly a member of the Body of Christ? They solved this problem in different ways, though each by using the word 'invisible'. Luther held that the exact composition of the Church of Christ was invisible, except to the eye of faith. There were hypocrites, heretics, unbelievers, and immoral persons within the outward Church, within the institution where the Gospel was preached and the Sacraments were administered; they did not belong to the Body of Christ, but only the eye of faith could identify them, and distinguish them from the true believers. In this sense, and in this sense only, Luther held the true Church to be invisible. For Calvin the doctrine of the invisible Church was bound up with the doctrine of predestination. God has chosen His Elect, and they form the true Church; but the company of the Elect is not co-terminous with the actual, visible, existing Church in any of its forms, reformed or unreformed, for many of the Elect are not members, and many of the members are not Elect. Therefore the Church as it truly is before God is invisible to men. Yet Calvin goes straight on, inconsistently perhaps, to assert his doctrine of the visible Church and to insist that abandonment of it is fatal; and he spends an infinitely greater amount of care in his writings, as he did in his life, on working out the nature of the visible Church than in laying down the doctrine of the invisible Church.

Individualistic tendencies in the Evangelical Revival, especially in its Anglican form, and in political and religious thought during the nineteenth century, combined with the constantly recurring problem of 'hypocrites within the Church', have frequently led Protestants to lay stress on the doctrine of the invisible Church, and to be less concerned with outward order and discipline, and with outward unity, than they should have been. But these defects can certainly not be charged against Luther and Calvin, and they do not belong to the essence of Protestantism. We are not in any sense bound by Calvin's doctrine of the invisible Church, now it has been found, in spite of the great authority of St Augustine as well as of Calvin, to be absent from Scripture. Most of us have, therefore, abandoned it, just as we have abandoned the doctrine of Predestination, at least as set out by Calvin. We are disposed to account for the presence of hypocrites in the Church (though not of sinners, for the Church is made up of sinners in process of being saved), not by saying that the true Church is invisible, but by saying that the Church on earth, though it is the Body of Christ and the Bride of Christ, is not yet what it will be, and therefore contains unworthy elements and unworthy people; it both is, and is not yet, the sanctified People of God. Only when it is set free from the limitations of time and space, and the yet graver limitations set by human sin, will the Church fully be what, in the purpose of God, it already is.

A Roman or Anglo-Catholic, reading this, would find it odd that we have said so much about the Church and so little about the Ministry, and he might conclude that we set little store by the ministerial structure of the Church. But he would be mistaken, even though it might, as so often, be our fault that he had made his error. We hold that the Church is prior to the Ministry, but we also hold that the Ministry is essential to the Church. It is, in fact, one of the direct gifts of Christ to His Church for the carrying on of the work which He Himself initiated and gave to the Church to continue. He gave this gift to the whole Church, which is, through and through, a 'royal priesthood, a holy nation, a people for God's own possession, that [we] may shew forth the excellencies of him who called [us] out of darkness into his marvellous light' (1 Peter 2⁹). This is the major part of our doctrine of the 'Priesthood of All Believers', so often narrowed down to be merely an assertion (true enough, of course), that every believer has the right of access, through Christ, to God. For Christ committed His own Ministry, both sacramental and evangelistic, to the whole body of His Church. He made the promises of His presence, He gave the commission to preach, He assigned the right to bind and to loose, to the Twelve, not as the first members of a self-perpetuating order within the Church, but as the nucleus, the representatives, of the whole Church of Christ, that is, of all who should believe through their preaching. And so what was given to them belongs to the whole Church; the whole Church possesses the apostolic, the essential ministry.

Within this greater ministry there are especial functions of discipline, administration, government, celebration of the sacraments, preaching the Word, and many others, of which St Paul several times gives us his list. To these offices men and women are called by the Church in the exercise of its ministry, and those duly called fulfil their offices on behalf of the whole Church. The New Testament lays down no rules for the ordering of the Church and its Ministry. There are traces of Presbyterianism, Independency, and Episcopalianism within the New Testament, and clearly the primitive Church did not settle a government either for itself or for the Church of the future. Nor can we take as determinative for all time the system of monarchical episcopacy which was developed during the second century, for it came into being to meet a series of emergencies, at a time when there was already a declension of life and doctrine from the zeal and purity of the New Testament's pattern of life for the Church. Therefore Protestants are committed to no particular form of Church government; Presbyterianism, Independency, and Episcopalianism are all allowable by the standards of the New Testament, and all, no doubt, have their place within the past, the present, and the future of the Church.

CHAPTER FIVE

Protestants and the Sacraments

ALL THE authoritative Protestant definitions of the Church which were quoted in the previous chapter mentioned the administration of the Sacraments as part of the essence of the Church. The Sacraments thus referred to are two: Holy Baptism and the Lord's Supper (variously known as the Eucharist and the Holy Communion). In each of the great Protestant communions the regular celebration of these sacraments is part of the structure of the Christian life; and each member of these communions is in the first place received into the Church by Baptism, and on attaining full or adult membership is in duty bound to receive the Communion regularly thereafter by the conditions of membership which he has accepted. We have to admit with sorrow that during the nineteenth century an opinion somehow gained currency within the British Free Churches that the Sacrament of the Lord's Supper, and even sometimes the Sacrament of Baptism, was in some way optional for Church members; and the evil effects of this non-Protestant, nineteenth-century-liberal notion have not entirely passed away from our Churches. But the formularies and traditions of these Churches have never given the slightest countenance to this aberration. Lutheranism has never been guilty of it. Calvin held that the Lord's Supper should be celebrated weekly (though he was later forced to agree to a less frequent celebration); one of the most striking results of the Methodist revival in eighteenth-century England was the enormous increase in those who wished to receive the Holy Communion, and there is a notable desire for more regular and more frequent Communions in all the British Free Churches at the present time.

The orders of service for the two Sacraments differ

widely throughout the Protestant Churches, but all insist in Baptism on the use of water and the Triune Name of God, and in the Holy Communion on repeating the narrative of the Last Supper and Christ's words of institution. The Lutheran rite in many countries is not markedly different from that of Rome, except that it is always in the vernacular, and expressions which are theologically obnoxious to Protestantism are omitted; Luther had no objection to the use of the word 'Mass', however, so long as it did not imply that the sacrifice of Christ was repeated or that we offered a sacrifice by which God's favour was secured. The Reformed, or Calvinistic, rites are notably simpler than those of the Lutheran tradition. Some of the English Free Churches prefer to use no set form at all; the Methodist Church, while allowing freedom to use no liturgy, authorizes two liturgies, one closely resembling, the other based on, the Order of Holy Communion in the *Book of Common Prayer*.

We speak of two Sacraments only in the full and proper sense, though we gratefully acknowledge the sacramental value of many acts of devotion, and not least that of the Marriage Service. Holy Baptism and Holy Communion are the two Sacraments of the Gospel, and that phrase is to be understood in two senses. In the first place, they are the Sacraments for the celebration of which we have the direct mandate of Christ Himself in the Gospels; the Christian Church cannot in conscience preach the Gospel without at the same time administering these two Sacraments. But there is a profounder sense in which they are the Sacraments of the Gospel: they preach and embody the Gospel. The Apostle Paul said of Holy Communion: 'As often as ye eat this bread and drink this cup ye proclaim the Lord's death until He come' (1 Cor. 11[26]), and the whole action of the Eucharist is an announcement of the suffering and death of Christ for our sins and of His triumph over sin by the Resurrection. Baptism also, and just as truly, proclaims the Gospel, for 'we were buried with Him through baptism unto death, that like as Christ was raised from the dead through the glory of the Father, so we also might walk in newness of life' (Romans 6⁴); thus it announces the power of God through Christ to bring about our death to sin and our rising again to the new life of righteousness. Or we can put this truth about the Sacraments in another way by saying that what the preacher proclaims in word about the Grace of God and the Death and Resurrection of Christ the Sacraments proclaim in deed. Some Churches place more emphasis on the preaching, some on the Sacraments; the Protestant Churches have tended to do the former rather than the latter, the Catholic Churches the latter rather than the former. In fact, however, the Word and Sacraments belong together, and a loss of the balance between them always leads to spiritual impoverishment.

The Sacraments are 'signs' and 'symbols' of the grace of God; but they are not bare signs, intended merely to remind us of something which has happened in the past, nor are they mere symbols, tokens of a reality which is truly present elsewhere. They are *effective* signs and *operative* symbols. Christ is the minister in the Sacrament of Baptism; it is He who receives the child or the adult into His Church; it is He who offers to him the gifts of forgiveness and new life in Him of which Baptism is the sign and seal. Christ is the host at His Supper; He has promised to be present whenever His followers receive the bread and wine which are the tokens of His Body and Blood; He seals afresh with us the New Covenant of His Blood; He makes available for us the 'innumerable benefits which by His precious blood-shedding He hath obtained for us'. We cannot believe that His presence is confined to the elements, or that the elements when taken out of the context of sacramental worship retain the qualities or remain the 'substance' of His Body and Blood. But we believe most firmly that He is really and truly present, giving us both spiritual food for this present life and a foretaste of the heavenly banquet which He has promised to those who love Him. In the words of one of Charles Wesley's eucharistic hymns:

C

We need not now go up to heaven,
   To bring the long-sought Saviour down;
Thou art to all already given,
   Thou dost e'en now Thy banquet crown:
To every faithful soul appear,
And show Thy real presence here.

We receive the sacramental gifts by faith. It is not only those who are especially good who can receive what God promises in His Sacraments; there is no requirement of goodness, but only of faith. Nor is it demanded of us that our faith should be perfect, or firm and secure beyond the reach of ordinary men and women, nor even that our faith should be strong at all. God honours the least movement of faith toward Him, both to forgive us our sins, and to bestow the gifts of Christ's Real Presence. For He takes our small and meagre offering of faith, and makes it by His Spirit the faith which receives His grace in simple gratitude and humility. 'We do not presume to come to this Thy table, O Lord, trusting in our own righteousness, but in Thy manifold and great mercies.' In the Baptism of infants it is the faith of the Church and of the parents or sponsors which receives the promises; in the Baptism of Believers it is the faith of the believer himself which does so. In the Holy Communion the promises are received by the faith of everyone who comes expecting to receive, and by the faith of the whole Church, which is present with the faithful, however few they are, at every celebration of the Lord's Supper. If a man comes without faith, the Sacrament may be for him a meaningless rite, and some would say with St Paul that he eats and drinks to his own destruction. Yet it is a matter of repeated experience that faith is aroused by the Sacrament itself in the minds of those who come without it; John Wesley frequently spoke of the Holy Communion as a 'converting ordinance'.

What has been said so far on the subject of the Sacraments would probably command the assent of practically all Protestants. It is well known, however, that there is difference of opinion among Protestants on various aspects of Sacramental doctrine. This is a matter not to be wondered at, nor yet to be deplored so long as it does not lead to divisions, as it sometimes has done; for the New Testament has no settled and firm doctrine of the Sacraments, and where the New Testament leaves us in doubt we have no right to lay down the law.

The deepest difference of opinion is on the subject of Baptism. The Churches in the Baptist tradition will not baptize infants, but only those who have shown their personal faith in Christ by public profession. They argue that there is no evidence for the practice of Infant Baptism in the New Testament; and they cannot fit the high sacramental doctrine of Baptism in the sixth chapter of the Epistle to the Romans to the Baptism of those who cannot think or decide for themselves. How can we say this of infants, they ask, 'We were buried with Him through Baptism into death: that like as Christ was raised from the dead through the glory of the Father, so we also might walk in newness of life'?

All other Protestants baptize infants brought for Baptism by those who will be responsible for bringing them up in the 'nurture and admonition of the Gospel'. They point out that the situation in the New Testament was a missionary situation, in which, naturally, those baptized were normally adults; and that St Paul's theology of Baptism applies to them. But since the early days of the Church, and perhaps already in New Testament times, the children of believers have been welcomed into the Church by Baptism, which places them within the realm of God's grace and prepares them to receive, after proper instruction and personal decision, the fullness of His forgiveness and favour.

This difference does not, however, prevent Protestants from taking communion together over most of the area of Protestant Christendom. There is, in fact, a very large degree of intercommunion between the members of the Protestant family. Some of the Lutheran Churches find themselves unable to come to the Lord's Table with those who do not hold the doctrine of Consubstantiation, which is that the substance of the Body and Blood of Christ is present in and with the substance of bread and wine after the words of consecration have been said; this doctrine is not held except in the Lutheran Churches. There are some Baptist Churches in the southern half of the United States who will not take communion with those who hold a non-Baptist view of Baptism. And Protestants within the Churches of the Anglican Communion are for the most part withheld from intercommunion with other Protestants by the practice of their own Church and the scruples of their Anglo-Catholic fellow Anglicans. For the rest, there is complete intercommunion.

We may be asked whether we regard the two Sacraments of the Gospel as necessary for salvation. We hold that Christ instituted these Sacraments, and that those who take His name are bound to honour His ordinances. But we do not consign to damnation those who for reasons of conscience (however wrongly held) or of ignorance are unwilling or unable to take them. For ourselves, we take God's gifts willingly and gladly. But God is free to save men by any means which He shall appoint. So we make Luther's maxim our own: God is not bound by His Sacraments; but we are.

I hope that the positive reasons why I am a Protestant have now appeared. They can be summarized in a sentence: I am a Protestant because I find that, of all forms of the Christian religion, Protestantism answers most nearly to the Word of God in Scripture. I do not believe that Protestantism has seen all the truth, or freed itself from every error; I am, I hope, willing to learn from the teaching and practice of every Church; and 'God hath yet more light and truth to break forth from His Word'. But I do believe that Scriptural truth is more fully and accurately expressed in the faith of Protestants than anywhere else in Christendom.

I come in Part Two to my negative reasons for being a Protestant. I shall try to show that Roman Catholicism, in spite of its greatness and its remarkable history, falls short of and conflicts with Scriptural truth in many vital places.

THE ROMAN CATHOLIC ALTERNATIVE

CHAPTER SIX

The Greatness of the Roman Church

WHEN PROTESTANTS write about the Church of Rome, they are tempted, no doubt by some obscure motive of self-defence, to dwell upon the evil things which Rome has done; and a similar tendency is not noticeably absent when Roman Catholics write about Protestantism. It will not be possible to avoid all mention of the evil deeds of Rome in this book, or to abstain from ascribing them to the inherent qualities of that Church; to do so would be to falsify history. And it would, of course, be an equal falsification to omit or deny the evil deeds of Protestants. But before we embark on criticism, attack, and defence, it is required by simple justice that we should pay sincere tribute to the greatness of that from which we profoundly dissent. Nor are we moved by considerations of justice alone; our Roman brethren, from whom we are separated, belong with us to the Body of Christ, and to refuse to recognize the gifts of God which have been granted to them would be a total failure in that 'love of the brethren' which the New Testament so frequently enjoins.

It is a little difficult to define the Roman Church. Probably the phrase calls up many different pictures in the minds of different readers. For present purposes it is best to define it as that part of the Christian Church throughout the ages which professes obedience to the See of Rome. The size and content of that part of the Church

have varied vastly from time to time. It may roughly
be said that until the end of the first century the authority
of the Bishop of Rome scarcely went beyond the limits of
the City of Rome; that in the second century it was ex-
tended to the rest of Italy, and was sometimes asserted
farther afield, but usually not acknowledged; that in the
third and fourth centuries the suzerainty of Rome was
accepted, at first in a rather vague way, but later with
closer definition, by nearly all the Churches in the
Western half of the Roman Empire—that is, in Italy,
North Africa (apart from Egypt), France, Spain, Britain,
the parts of Germany which were under Roman control,
and the area now covered by Yugoslavia. In the fifth
century the City of Rome itself sank into a position of
inferiority in relation to Constantinople, and even sometimes in relation to some of the other great cities of the
Western Empire; but, by one of the paradoxes of history, the power of the Church of Rome grew while that
of the City declined. At the end of the century Pope
Gregory the Great was acknowledged not only as the
head of the Western Church, but, over wide areas, as
the head of the Eastern Church, that is, of the Church
of the Eastern Empire, as well. 'Who can doubt', Gregory
was able to say, 'that the Church of Constantinople is
subject to the Apostolic See?'

The position of the Pope in relation to the Churches
of the Eastern Empire was never, however, made perfectly clear; and there were only short periods during
which his supremacy was recognized there. It is safest,
on historical grounds, to exclude the Eastern Churches
from the definition of the Church of Rome, though the
final repudiation of its authority did not come, perhaps,
until the thirteenth century.[1] Until then, the Eastern
patriarchs were willing to give honour to the Church of
Rome, though not greater authority to its Bishops than

[1] The date of the final split between East and West is usually given as
1054; but there is now strong reason for supposing that relations of a
more or less friendly kind continued until the sack of Constantinople by
the Crusaders in 1203. (See S. Runciman, *The Eastern Schism* (1955).)

they themselves possessed. But in the West the power of the Papacy grew steadily from the time of Gregory, who died in 604, until that of Pope Nicholas the Great (858-67), who was able to appoint and depose Bishops against the will of the Holy Roman Emperor himself. The pontificate of Nicholas was followed by a period of internal decay within the Papacy itself, and although the Papal authority over the Church in the West was not officially questioned, it was not effectively exercised. In the twelfth century, the genius of Hildebrand, the adviser of many Popes, and later Pope himself under the name of Gregory VII, reasserted and regained for the Papacy the authority which it had largely lost, and from his time until the Reformation in the sixteenth century the Bishop of Rome was the unquestioned head of the Church in the West. The sixteenth century saw the departure of most of Northern Europe from the Papal allegiance; but this loss has been offset in the subsequent centuries by the gain of South America and the establishment of powerful Roman Catholic Churches in the lands of missionary enterprise and in the United States.

Until the Reformation, what we now call Protestantism was comprehended within the Roman Church, which was then Protestant as well as Catholic: Protestantism is as old as the New Testament, and has a full and continuous history from the time of the Apostles; the early Franciscans, for instance, were the Methodists of the twelfth century. Roman Catholicism has no greater claim to antiquity than Protestantism. Thus it is wrong to speak of the Church of the Middle Ages as the Roman Catholic Church, or of St Benedict or St Dominic or St Bernard of Clairvaux as Roman Catholic saints. They are Saints of the Church, to which Protestants have always belonged, and of what for convenience we call the Roman Church (as distinct from the Roman Catholic Church) in particular, to which until the Reformation all Protestants in Western Christendom belonged. The Roman Catholic Church was the result of the Reformation, and the creation of the Council of Trent, which met from 1545 to

1563. The Roman Catholic Church is that part of the previous Roman Church which retained its obedience to the Pope; it is the 'Roman Church Continuing'.

The Roman Church, thus defined, is certainly the most remarkable institution in the whole history of religion, and probably the most remarkable institution in the whole of human history. Its Christian achievements began when the Bishops of Rome in the centuries of persecution by the Roman State maintained a steadfastness in danger and a grasp of Scriptural truth which were an example and an inspiration to the whole of the Church. When the political power of imperial Rome tottered and fell, the Pope took the place of the Emperor in all men's minds as the focus of Roman loyalty, and built up in the minds of Christians a permanent and well-founded reputation as the guardian of spiritual security and unity, and of continuity with the past. While fierce and immature nations, in what we call the Dark Ages, battled over the corpse and estate of the Roman Empire, the Church of Rome was the bulwark of civilization as well as of Christianity, and gradually subdued the barbarians to obedience to her Canon Law and to at least an outward observance of Christian commandments and respect for Christian culture. When the kings of the Franks bade fair to become the masters of Europe, the Popes saw to it that the Roman Empire which Charles the Great was aspiring to restore should be a Holy, a Christian Empire.

From the point of view of the political historian, the Middle Ages are one long struggle between the Empire and the Papacy for predominance in the affairs of Europe, and the part played by political and personal ambition in the purposes and plans of Popes cannot be honestly neglected. Yet at the same time the Roman Church was giving to Europe a unity of theological thought, of devotion and worship, of ethical standard and public law, of spiritual administration and intellectual endeavour, which never became a dull uniformity, but produced a harmony of outlook and attitude among the nations for which

European statesmen and churchmen would give the world today. Greatest of all its medieval achievements was the intellectual activity of the Schoolmen which it sponsored and which gave to the thinkers of the whole continent a synthesis of all existing knowledge under the aegis of the Queen of the Sciences, theology.

These may be reckoned as the outward achievements of a great religious organization. What of the inner life of its members? There were, no doubt, long periods in the Dark and Middle Ages of sterility and corruption, even among the official professors of the 'religious life'; but the monastic communities of Europe, owing their primary inspiration to St Martin of Tours (336-401) and their organization to St Benedict of Nursia (480-543), maintained a fire of devotion and piety which sometimes burned low, though it was never quite put out, and sometimes burned with dazzling brightness amid the surrounding darkness. Then at the beginning of the thirteenth century came the Franciscans and the Dominicans to preach to the poor, to teach the ignorant and misguided, to heal and comfort the afflicted and the sorrowful, bringing the truths of the monastery into the lives of ordinary men and women. From the ranks of the monks and the friars came all, or nearly all, the individuals who have struck the imagination of succeeding generations by their powers of thought, their statesmanship, their mystical insight, their love of mankind, and their holiness of life; and from the same quarter came the treasure of devotional literature which Protestantism has never been able to equal in spiritual depth and range.

Since the Reformation, the Roman Church (now the Roman Catholic Church), though deprived of its Protestant members and of great areas of spiritual and intellectual influence, has yet not ceased to add to the record of its greatness. She has as much reason to be proud of her martyrs and saints as the Protestant Churches have to be proud of theirs. The Jesuit and other Roman missionaries have gone to the far corners of the earth, well in advance of their Protestant brethren, and confirmed their work by flourishing communities in every continent and almost every country. Her philosophers and theologians, though confined within the somewhat narrow limits of the Tridentine, and later the Vatican, Decrees, have yet shown the continuing vitality of the Scholastic mode of thought and have made contributions to the study of individual doctrines and periods of history which take rank with anything that Protestantism has produced; and in recent years her biblical scholars have begun to take an honoured place alongside those of Protestant Christianity. Warned by the Reformation and strengthened by the Counter-Reformation, her monastic communities have restored the ancient purity of their life; and there has been no lack of individual 'religious' men and women to inspire the rest, and indirectly the whole Christian world, by their example and their writings.

When the Nazi tyranny in Germany began to threaten the very vitals of the Church, Roman Catholic cardinals, bishops, priests, and people offered resistance as obstinate, effective, and sacrificial as that of the Protestant Confessing Church. Militant Communism regards the Church of Rome, with its world-wide organization and power, as the chief religious obstacle to its establishment of the universal dictatorship of the proletariat, and history so far has done much to validate this judgement.

We give thanks to God for the Christian graces of the martyrs, saints, heroes, thinkers, statesmen, and faithful men and women of the Roman Church, including those who in sincere obedience to their conscience and the truth as it was taught by their Church have opposed and sought to destroy the Protestant faith.

CHAPTER SEVEN

The Truths Taught by the Roman Catholic Church

WE SHALL be obliged, in the following chapters of this book, to point out and confute the errors of the Roman Catholic Church. But here we need to say that alongside these errors exists a large body of Christian truth. It is no part of the Protestant case against Rome to claim that she is sunk in total error, or to refuse to recognize and acknowledge with gratitude the amount of biblical truth which she has retained in spite of all temptations to corruption and superstition. It is worth remembering that large parts of Christian doctrine were not discussed in the Reformation period, simply because the Reformers had no reason to think that the Roman Church had fallen into error about them.

We have seen that the Nicene Creed is a trustworthy summary of the faith of the New Testament. It is accepted by Catholics and Protestants alike, except of course that the Orthodox Churches repudiate the addition of the words 'and the Son' to the statement that the Holy Spirit proceeds from the Father. To the Nicene Creed the Roman Church has remained unswervingly loyal throughout its history, and no charge of betraying Scriptural truth can plausibly be brought against its doctrines on any of the Persons of the Trinity, the one Baptism, the Resurrection of the Dead, or the Life of the World to Come. In fact, the only phrase in the Creed which engages the Protestant and Catholic sections of the Church in permanent controversy is that which concerns the 'one, holy, catholic, and apostolic Church'. Here the difference concerns only the matter of interpretation; the article of faith is acceptable to all. The Roman Catholic Church, by identifying the one, holy, catholic, and apostolic Church with that part of Christendom which acknowledges the supremacy of the Bishop of Rome, that is, with itself, seems to Protestants to be going far outside the possible meaning of Scripture. But this is the only error of which it is guilty in respect of the Nicene Creed.

We can go farther than this. The Roman Catholic Church not only professes its faith in the Creed; it probably takes the Creed more seriously and teaches it more assiduously than any other part of the Christian Church. Roman Catholic peasants have through the ages been allowed to remain in a state of ignorance, and often superstition, about the articles of their faith. But the educated Roman Catholic today, at least in those countries where Protestantism is strong, has normally been much better instructed in the doctrines of the Creed than his counterpart in the Protestant Churches.

Nor are the truths taught by the Roman Catholic Church limited to those which are set out in the Nicene Creed. In at least three other important respects the Roman Church has been, and the Roman Catholic Church still is, the vigilant guardian of common Christian truth. Against the Gnostics of the second century, the Manichaeans of the third century, and the successors of both these groups in later centuries, all of them maintaining that the human body and the natural, physical life of man are undilutedly evil, the Roman Church asserted that God is the Creator of flesh as well as spirit; and it thus preserved the whole of Christendom on many occasions from falling a victim to the oriental ideas which were constantly filtering into Christian thought. The notion that Rome defended the bodily life of man may strike oddly on some Protestant ears, which have grown accustomed to tales of monks and nuns who utterly denied the value of marriage and family life, and it is true that Manichaeism, or something very like it, has sometimes disguised itself very successfully as the fulfilment of Christ's 'counsels of perfection'. But in all its official pronouncements Rome has steadfastly set its face against undue asceticism, and encouraged the ordinary man to live his ordinary life within his family in obedience to the law of Christ. It is true that it has largely achieved this end by enunciating the doctrine of the 'double standard', by which those who aim at perfection renounce all bodily pleasures and satisfactions, and those who do not aim so high are encouraged to marry and raise families; and Protestantism has much more effectively reclaimed the life of the body by asserting one law of Christ for all men. Yet it remains true that until the Reformation, in spite of all abuses, the Roman Church resisted with might and main every attempt of so-called spiritual religion within and without the Church to damn our body of mortal flesh.

Secondly, the Roman Church has been in the past, and the Roman Catholic Church still is, the champion of human reason. Once the principal dogmas of the Church have been accepted on authority, the Roman Catholic has been not only allowed, but also encouraged, to think out his faith, and its relations to other parts of human knowledge, to the utmost of his powers in company with the profoundest thinkers whom he can consult. This may again sound strange to Protestants, who have always supposed that the priest leaves his flock in a state of deepest ignorance in order to perpetuate and increase his own power; and certainly that is what seems to happen to unlettered people in predominantly Roman Catholic countries. But the educated man and the intellectual receive a very different treatment; and the theologians and teachers of the Roman Catholic Church are compelled to submit themselves to as rigid a mental discipline as is to be found in any university in the world. This emphasis has sometimes, in fact, been carried to extremes: Luther certainly made out his case when he charged the learned theologians of his time with fitting Christianity into a pre-conceived intellectual system; and the highly dubious notion that the existence of God can be entirely demonstrated by argument has been exalted in Rome almost to the status of a dogma. But these excesses do not affect the fact that Rome can rightly claim to be the champion of reason, not least against the irrationalism that sometimes becomes fashionable in Protestant circles.

Finally, the Roman Church contended unremittingly, and the Roman Catholic Church still contends, for the absolute priority of the supernatural order over the natural. In the first centuries after the end of persecution, she avoided the Caesaro-Papalism, the submission of Church to Emperor, which has dogged the footsteps of the Orthodox Churches ever since the time of the Emperor Theodosius at the end of the fourth century. In the Dark Ages she herself often dominated the secular scene in the interests, officially, of the supernatural order, though often, it is to be feared, of her own. In the Middle Ages she never allowed the secular power to usurp the rights of the Church, except when her rulers were so degraded or so weak as to be untrue to their own loudly proclaimed policy. In the modern period she has, on the whole, escaped that overclose identification with established government which has ruined so much Protestant witness. And even today, when she speaks, men who repudiate her authority and doubt the truth of her utterances are compelled to listen, in case they should hear some word from the Author of our being. For all her failures, for all her betrayals of the truth, for all her descents to the standards of the world which she presumes to judge, the Roman Catholic Church still bears vestiges of her ancient, proud position as guardian on earth of eternal truth and champion of everlasting law. Perhaps it is because of this that intelligent men of our time, who would find it very hard to believe her doctrines if they were presented with them one by one, nevertheless give to her their total submission, and believe what she commands them to believe.

But though she has guarded many truths, she has, alas, also nourished many errors; and some of these are so serious that it is impossible for anyone who has honestly studied the New Testament without previously submitting to her claims to believe that she is a trustworthy guide to the fullness of Christian truth.

To these errors we now turn.

CHAPTER EIGHT

St Peter and the Popes

'WE THEREFORE teach and declare that, according to the testimony of the Gospel, the primacy of jurisdiction over the universal Church was immediately and directly promised and given to blessed Peter the Apostle by Christ the Lord. . . . That which the Prince of Shepherds and great Shepherd of the sheep, Jesus Christ our Lord, established in the person of the blessed Apostle Peter to secure the perpetual welfare and lasting good of the Church, must, by the same institution, necessarily remain unceasingly in the Church; which, being founded upon the Rock, will stand firm to the end of the world. For none can doubt, and it is known to all ages, that the holy and blessed Peter, the Prince and Chief of the Apostles, the pillar of the faith and foundation of the Catholic Church, received the keys of the kingdom from our Lord Jesus Christ, the Saviour and Redeemer of mankind, and lives, presides, and judges, to this day and always, in his successors the Bishops of the Holy See of Rome, which was founded by him, and consecrated by his blood. Whence, whosoever succeeds to Peter in this See, does by the institution of Christ himself obtain the Primacy of Peter over the whole Church.'

This, from the first and second chapters of the *First Dogmatic Constitution on the Church of Christ of the Vatican Council of 1870*, states plainly and unequivocally the Roman Catholic doctrine of the primacy of the See of Rome, which is therefore an article of faith for all Roman Catholics. On what Scriptural and other arguments is it founded?

It is argued, first, that the New Testament in general plainly gives to St Peter pre-eminence over the other Apostles. Secondly, that three texts in particular (Matthew

16^{15-19}, John 21^{15-17}, Luke 22^{31-2}) show that Christ appointed Peter to a position of primacy in the Church. Thirdly, that Peter, as co-founder with Paul of the Church of Rome and its first Bishop, exercised his primacy in the See of Rome. And finally, that Peter transmitted his primacy to each of his successors as Bishop of Rome. The word 'primacy' is further defined in the Dogmatic Decrees of the Vatican Council as the 'full power to rule, feed, and govern the universal Church'.

We shall deal with these arguments one by one. The first states that the New Testament gives to Peter preeminence over the other Apostles, on the grounds, among others, that Peter is mentioned on over one hundred and ninety occasions, whereas St John, who comes next among the original Twelve, is mentioned only twenty-nine times; that Peter was the first apostle to be appointed; and that he consistently took the lead in any action of the Apostles both before and after the Crucifixion. The theologians of the Roman Catholic Church would not claim that this argument, in itself, does more than establish a primacy of honour, not jurisdiction, for Peter in the early Church. We grant that a fairly good case has been made out for such a primacy of honour, but by no means an irrefragable one. The number of times that St Peter is mentioned, for example, proves very little indeed, especially when we remember that St Paul, whose name may not be mentioned so often, actually wrote a considerable proportion of the New Testament, so that his personality, if not his name, is stamped upon it much more unmistakably than St Peter's. We should remember, too, when we are thinking about leadership, that at the Council of Jerusalem, described in Acts 15, it was St James, not St Peter, who presided. But we may readily admit that, in the Gospels at least, St Peter is honoured above his brethren, though he was also the Apostle most liable to make mistakes.

But what jurisdiction was he granted by Christ? Here 'the great Petrine texts' must bear all the weight, and of the three, the first, Matthew 16^{15-19}, is far and away the

most important. If this will not prove what it is claimed
to prove, the other two cannot come to the rescue. They
constitute the commands to St Peter, after he has be-
trayed his Lord and found forgiveness, to feed Christ's
lambs and sheep (John 21$^{15-17}$) and to confirm his brethren (Luke 22$^{31-2}$). Clearly, no unique commission is
given to St Peter in the words of these two passages alone;
though, if Jesus has already given to St Peter a unique
commission in the words of Matthew 16$^{15-19}$, these addi-
tional commands bear great significance.

We look, then, at Matthew 16$^{15-19}$: 'Simon Peter
answered and said, Thou art the Christ, the Son of the
living God. And Jesus answered and said unto him,
Blessed art thou, Simon Bar-Jonah: for flesh and blood
hath not revealed it unto thee, but my Father which is
in heaven. And I also say unto thee, that thou art Peter,
and upon this rock I will build my church; and the gates
of Hades shall not prevail against it. I will give unto
thee the keys of the kingdom of heaven: and whatsoever
thou shalt bind on earth shall be bound in heaven: and
whatsoever thou shalt loose on earth shall be loosed in
heaven' (RV).

It has often been seriously questioned whether the
words in this passage from 'And I also say unto thee' to
the end are the genuine words of Jesus. Their authenticity cannot be accepted unhesitatingly; for they occur
only in the Gospel of Matthew, and passages which are
peculiar to that Gospel must be treated with some slight
reserve; they include the word 'church', which is not
characteristic of the language of Jesus, and is only ascribed
to Him in one other place, Matthew 18^{17}, a passage also
peculiar to Matthew's Gospel; and the phrase 'the keys
of the kingdom of heaven' implies a meaning for the
'kingdom of heaven' very different from that which Jesus
gives to it in every other place in which He speaks of it.
But these considerations are not strong enough to do
more than throw some doubt on the authenticity of the
passage.

But if we assume that Jesus actually uttered the words

in question, what is 'this rock'? The Roman Catholic case depends, to an extent which ought to be alarming to every Roman Catholic, on its being St Peter himself. But this is only one of many possible interpretations. The Fathers suggest and adopt several. Only seventeen of them understand the rock as St Peter himself; forty-four interpret it as the faith confessed by him; eight as all the Apostles; sixteen as Christ Himself. St Augustine wavered between the first and second interpretations. The modern reader, remaining as open-minded as he can, will be tempted to follow the example of St Augustine and leave the matter open—until he remembers that Matthew tells us that a few days later the disciples came and asked Jesus the very question which Rome claims to have been settled once and for all at Caesarea Philippi in the words about the rock: they asked, Who is greatest in the kingdom of heaven? (Matthew 18[1]). Surely it is inconceivable that the disciples should have asked this question, of all questions, if Jesus had just saluted St Peter as the rock on which the Church is built? This passage puts it almost beyond doubt that the 'rock' is the faith of St Peter, not St Peter himself, and the play on the word 'Peter' (or 'Cephas'), meaning a 'stone' or 'rock', is as well maintained by this interpretation as by the Roman Catholic one. The question asked by the disciples in Matthew 18[1] not only helps us to determine the meaning of the 'rock passage'; it also shows, surely, that when Jesus gave to St Peter 'the keys of the kingdom of heaven' He was not giving them to him exclusively, but to him as representing, for the time being, the whole Church. This is strongly borne out by the fact that the power 'to bind and loose', which is here given to St Peter, is in Matthew 18[18] given to all the Apostles. In other words, in this whole passage, St Peter is not singled out by himself alone for especial honour and power; he is treated as the representative of the Apostles and the Church because he has, in the words, 'Thou art the Christ, the Son of the living God', spoken the faith of them all.

If this argument is sound, or if only that part of it is sound which relates to the 'rock', the case of Rome for the primacy of St Peter falls to the ground. But even if it is not, Rome has to build her whole case for St Peter's primacy on one particular interpretation of one particular passage—and that particular interpretation, to say the least of it, is by no means certain.

But let us assume, in order that we may continue the argument, that Christ did give the primacy to St Peter. What shall we make of the claim that he exercised it in the See of Rome as co-founder and bishop of the Church there? No one is concerned to doubt or deny that St Peter spent some part of his life there, or that he was martyred there. What is denied is that he was the co-founder of the Church there, and what is very seriously doubted is that he was the bishop of that Church.

Our earliest evidence about the Church of Rome comes from St Paul's Epistle to the Romans, written, almost certainly, in A.D. 58-9. The whole tone of this letter shows that St Paul had never himself visited the Church in Rome. Thus he himself is ruled out as co-founder with St Peter from the start. But there is no reference to St Peter either, or indeed to any founder. An argument from silence is said to be unreliable; but, in this case, since the primary purpose of the letter is to commend the author's Gospel and person to the Romans, the absence of reference to St Peter, if he was the founder of the Church, is quite unbelievable. It is the unanimous judgement of non-Roman Catholic interpreters, and it seems the obvious and necessary one, that the Church of Rome had no apostolic founder, but was brought into existence by Christians engaged in trade or coming to take up residence in the city.

Furthermore, there is good ground for supposing that there was already a Christian Church in Rome in A.D. 49. In that year, according to the Roman historian Suetonius, the Emperor Claudius 'expelled the Jews from Rome because they kept rioting at the instigation of Chrestus', and by far the most likely interpretation of this passage is that there had been trouble in the Roman synagogues between Christians and Jews; for 'Chrestus' is a very common mis-spelling for 'Christus', and this is just the kind of mistake that an ill-informed non-Christian would make. But if there were Christians in Rome in A.D. 49, St Peter cannot have founded their Church, for it is impossible to work out a plausible chronology of his life that allows him to have been in Rome as early as this.

There is a strong tradition from the second half of the second century that St Peter was the co-founder of the Church in Rome, but it cannot be held to offset the evidence that we have given on the other side. It is easy to see how the tradition arose. 'Other Churches had apostolic founders; surely Rome, mighty Rome, must have had one too? We know that St Peter and St Paul both taught in Rome, and suffered there. They must have been the founders of the Church.' To us, perhaps, not a plausible argument; but to a Roman Christian of the second century, very attractive indeed.

St Peter, then, did not found, or help to found, the Church of Rome. But was he its bishop? The modern Roman Catholic claim is not that he was ever actually called the Bishop of Rome, for it is now generally agreed that monarchical episcopacy, that is, the rule of a Church by one man, is not to be found in the Churches of the New Testament period, but was a second-century development; and it is acknowledged that Clement of Rome, writing in A.D. 96, makes no reference to a chief minister in Rome and does not speak as if he were a chief minister himself (though in later tradition he is called the 'bishop'). It is rather claimed that since St Peter lived as an Apostle in Rome, he must have exerted authority there identical with the authority later exercised by those who were called bishops. And, of course, it is further claimed that, since the primacy over the whole Church resided in St Peter, he must have exercised it from Rome.

The answer to this is that we really do not know what

St Peter did in Rome, how long he lived there, or what authority he exercised; nor has any good historical evidence ever been adduced to throw light on these points. There is no ascription of any episcopal title or authority to St Peter before the third century, and the earliest lists of Roman bishops starts with Linus, and not with either St Peter or St Paul. All we can say is that, if St Peter really exercised authority of the kind suggested, he must have spent a fairly long period of time in Rome. (For he visited many other Churches as well, and if only a brief visit sufficed for St Peter to be regarded as the bishop of a Church, many Churches could make the claim for their bishops which Rome has made for hers.) But there is just no evidence of any kind to show that he did make a fairly long stay. We can hardly be expected, therefore, to take very seriously this third argument for the primacy of the See of Rome.

The fourth argument is that St Peter transmitted his primacy over the whole Church to his successors as Bishop of Rome. If, of course, he never was Bishop of Rome in any proper sense, there can be no question of his transmitting any primacy to his successors; and some Roman Catholic apologists, conscious of the weakness of the case for St Peter's episcopate in Rome, have said that all he did was to 'deposit the primacy in the See of Rome'.[1] To this we can say that, for all that we know to the contrary, he might have deposited it in the See of Corinth, or some other See, and we should really like some evidence, which we have not been given, that it was in the See of Rome that it was deposited. But let us assume, again for the sake of argument, that St Peter had the primacy referred to, and was, in some sense, bishop of Rome, by what entitlement and on what ground did St Peter transmit to a line of unknown successors what Christ had given to him personally, and given to him on the ground of his own personal confession of faith? There is no evidence in Scripture that any transmission of any authority was authorized or countenanced by the Lord,

[1] Abbot John Chapman in *Bishop Gore and the Catholic Claims* (1905), p. 61.

least of all such vast authority as this. Can any reasonable man, not overwhelmed by the prestige of the Roman Church, with the silence of Scripture shouting in his ears, believe that Jesus intended this full-orbed sovereignty over the whole of His Church to be handed down in this way, or to be handed down at all? And what evidence have we that St Peter did so hand it down? Perhaps the finally conclusive fact is that it was not until A.D. 256 that the Roman Church itself claimed for its bishop the primacy of St Peter; the Pope had apparently received this primacy nearly two hundred years before, but he never thought to mention it!

The Roman Church's claim to the universal primacy of its bishop can be buttressed by the historical achievements of many Popes, and by the acknowledgement of the Pope as the Head of the Church by many Christian countries. But its foundation in Scripture, in the history of the primitive Church, and in reason, is non-existent. As we have seen, the grounds on which it is urged are the dubious interpretation of a possibly non-authentic passage from the Gospels, one falsely alleged and one doubtfully alleged event in the life of St Peter, and the unvouched-for exercise of a power by St Peter which there is no reason to think that he possessed.

CHAPTER NINE

The Basic Error

'THEREFORE FAITHFULLY adhering to the tradition received from the beginning of the Christian faith, for the glory of God our Saviour, the exaltation of the Catholic religion, and the salvation of Christian people, the sacred Council approving, we teach and define that it is a dogma divinely revealed: that the Roman Pontiff, when he speaks *ex cathedra*, that is, when in discharge of the office of pastor and doctor of all Christians, by virtue of his supreme Apostolic authority, he defines a doctrine regarding faith or morals to be held by the universal Church, by the divine assistance promised to him in blessed Peter, is possessed of that infallibility with which the divine Redeemer willed that his Church should be endowed for defining doctrine regarding faith or morals; and that therefore such definitions of the Roman Pontiff are irreformable of themselves, and not from the consent of the Church.'

This is the last part of the last chapter, which is entitled 'Concerning the Infallible Teaching of the Roman Pontiff', of the *First Dogmatic Constitution of the Church of Christ of the Vatican Council of 1870*. It is, of course, a matter of faith of all Roman Catholics. It was framed with scrupulous and long-continued care, after much controversy and reflection; and it deserves to be read and studied with equal care. It should be noticed at once that the exercise of the Pope's infallibility is very strictly limited to those occasions when he speaks *ex cathedra*, that is, when he defines a doctrine regarding faith or morals to be held by the universal Church, and does so in discharge of the office of pastor and doctor of all Christians. There is no suggestion that the Pope is infallible when he speaks on ordinary, secular matters, or even when he gives general guidance on matters of faith or morals, but only when he 'defines a doctrine' as 'pastor and doctor of all Christians'.

But however circumscribed it may be, how entirely alien is any claim to infallibility to the whole teaching and spirit of the New Testament! Contrast with it such sayings as: 'We know in part, and we prophesy in part' (1 Corinthians 13⁹); 'we walk by faith, not by sight' (2 Corinthians 5⁷). In the New Testament the Church itself stands under the judgement of God, and must at all times lie open to His correction, even though it has the commission of Christ to preach the Gospel to every creature, and even though Christ has imparted to it the knowledge of God; judgement is to 'begin at the house of God' (1 Peter 4¹⁷). and not the greatest teacher, not the purest saint, is exempt from it. Nor were the Apostles free from error. St Paul himself changed his teaching on various subjects during the time when he was writing the Epistles, notably on the Second Coming and the life of the world to come. St Peter was publicly rebuked for error by St Paul (Galatians 2¹¹), as he had previously been rebuked by Jesus Himself, and it was the teaching and practice of St Paul, not those of St Peter, that were upheld at the Council of Jerusalem, St Peter himself having by that time come round to St Paul's view (Acts 15¹⁻²¹).[1]

The life of the Christian and the Church, according to all the teaching of the New Testament, is a life, not of intellectual certainty about spiritual issues and problems, but of personal trust in Christ, enabling us to rely utterly on God, but not to claim knowledge of all His secrets, or complete and infallible knowledge of any one of them. We are His creatures and His children; we have not the minds to grasp the fullness of His mind or of His purposes even in the smallest particular, still less concerning universal truth. Nor is there the slightest evidence in the New Testament that God overrides the limitations of a human mind, even the mind of St Peter

[1] This presumes that the events of Galatians 2 preceded those of Acts 15. If they followed them, St Peter was in error *after* the Council of Jerusalem.

or St Paul, to implant a truth which it cannot understand. Such an action would be quite contrary to all His known methods of dealing with the human soul, for He always respects our personality, even our weakness of understanding and imagination. His work in us is never overwhelming, overruling, repressive of our minds and selves; it is always a gracious, personal relationship.

All kinds of infallibility are, therefore, ruled out by the New Testament from the start; the notion of infallibility is, in the last resort, Islamic, not biblical. We can turn upside down the traditional Roman argument for infallibility that says: *potuit, decuit, ergo fecit*—He was able, it was right for Him, therefore He did it. It is blasphemous to suggest that we know what was 'right for Him' to do, unless we have Scriptural warrant; and here we have none. We say rather: *potuit, sed non decuit, ergo non fecit*— He was able, but it was not right for Him, therefore He did not do it. For we know from Scripture that He does not deem it right to override the human spirit and destroy the conditions on which He has enacted that human life should be lived.

But let us follow the same procedure as was used in the previous chapter. Let us, for the sake of argument, suppose that God does grant infallibility to certain people for certain purposes. How can we possibly know when He has done so and to whom He has granted it? Setting aside the minor sects of apocalyptic Christianity, all of whom have a doctrine of infallibility as rigid as that of Rome, we have several formidable claimants for the position of 'infallible teacher of Christian truth'; and if any one of these makes good its claim, the claims of the others fall to the ground, for all the claimants contradict each other on vital points of doctrine. In particular, we have the Roman Catholic Church, with the Pope as its spokesman, the Orthodox Churches of the East (which all profess the same doctrine, so that their claims can be regarded, with complete fairness to them, as a single claim), the fundamentalists, who hold that the whole Bible, as the 'inspired Word of God', is infallible, and those who believe in the inerrancy of the Inner Light. All of us, no doubt, have our private views as to which of these comes nearest to the truth about the universe. But this, of course, is not the point. The point is: which of them, if any, is really infallible? If there is no way of determining this question, the claims of one and all are otiose and futile, and are not worth discussing any further. If there *is* a way of determining the question, it must be by the use of some insight or understanding or other divine gift which is itself infallible. For if I do not know infallibly that the Roman Catholic Church, or the Bible, is infallible, the knowledge which I have does not confer on me the benefits which would derive from my accepting an infallible authority; I am no nearer to an exact knowledge of the truth than I was before, and I am not in a position to state, as an article of Christian truth, that the Roman Catholic Church, or the Pope, is infallible. I simply give my own strong personal opinion to this effect. In particular, the Vatican Council, unless it was itself granted infallibility, could not pronounce the infallibility of the Pope. And, of course, if the Vatican Council was granted infallibility, how shall we know that either? We are launched on the same set of questions about its infallibility as about the infallibility of anything, or anyone, else, and so on, *ad infinitum*.

Abbot B. C. Butler, in his book *The Church and Infallibility*, one of the most reasonably argued books yet written to support the Roman Catholic doctrine, seeks to escape from the haunting circularity of the Roman Catholic argument for the infallibility of the Pope by saying that we know that the Pope is infallible not *infallibly*, but *certainly*. He distinguishes certainty and infallibility in the words of J. H. Newman (who uses 'certitude' for what Abbot Butler calls 'certainty'): 'I remember for certain what I did yesterday, but still my memory is not infallible; I am quite certain that two and two make four, but I often make mistakes in long addition sums. . . . A certitude is directed to this or that particular proposition, it is not a faculty or gift, but a disposition of mind relative to a definite case which is before me. Infallibility, on the contrary, is just what certitude is not; it *is* a faculty or gift, and relates, not to some one truth in particular, but to all possible propositions in a given subject-matter. . . . I may be certain that the Church is infallible, while I am myself a fallible mortal.'[1]

Thus, Abbot Butler argues, I may be certain that the Pope, or the Church, is infallible, without being infallible myself. But this certainty, though limited to the particular proposition under discussion, is apparently free from the possibility of error; it is thus open to the general objections to infallibility derived from Scripture, and to all the others, which we have already urged. Moreover, it does not help a man in the least who wishes to decide between the spokesmen of the various claimants to infallibility; for each one who puts forward such a claim is as certain that he is right as any of the rest; and when we come to test the certainty of a man who accepts the Roman claim, how are we to know that he is right and the others are wrong? Certainty and infallibility may be two different things, but the distinction between them does not assist the infallibility of the Pope.

But let us suppose, again for the sake of continuing the argument, that a *prima facie* case has been made out for regarding the Pope as infallible within the limits of the Vatican Council's decree. Does the study of Church History bear out the claim that the Pope has in fact been infallible? Two Popes, Vigilius (537-55) and Honorius (625-40), can be plainly shown to have erred in declaration of doctrine, both by Scripture and by the decrees of General Councils. Vigilius was appointed Pope by the personal influence of the Emperor Justinian. Justinian in 544 anathematized a set of books known as the *Three Chapters* (written by Theodore of Mopsuestia, who died in 428, Theodoret and Ibas) on the score that they propounded the Nestorian heresy. Shortly afterwards, in 548, Pope Vigilius publicly repeated the anathematization. Confronted with fierce opposition in the

---

[1] *The Church and Infallibility*, pp. 42-9.

Western Church, which held that an attack on the *Three Chapters* was an attack on the *Definition of Chalcedon*, Vigilius withdrew his anathematization. The fifth General Council, assembled at Constantinople in 553, condemned the *Three Chapters* lock, stock, and barrel. Some months later the Pope, confessing that he had been deceived by the Devil, withdrew his withdrawal of his anathematization, and avowed with fervour the anathematization of the *Three Chapters* by the fifth General Council. He died in ignominy.

Now it is true that the Roman Catholic Church treats the doctrinal pronouncements of Vigilius as *not* having been uttered *ex cathedra*, within the meaning of the Vatican Decree; but that Decree was drawn up with full recollection of the mistakes of Vigilius, and therefore was, of course, so framed that his statements did not need to be regarded as *ex cathedra* pronouncements. If, however, Vigilius had the power of infallibility, as on Roman doctrine we must suppose that he had, what right have we to say that he was not exercising it when he was defining a doctrine on faith or morals, as he undoubtedly was when he reinstated the *Three Chapters*? In his official letter to the Emperor, known as the *Constitutum*, he uses the word 'define' of what he was doing, and concludes: 'If anything has been already done or spoken in regard of the *Three Chapters* in contradiction of this our ordinance, by any one whomsoever, this we declare void by authority of the Apostolic See.'

The second example is that of Pope Honorius, who was asked his opinion in 634 by Sergius, Patriarch of Jerusalem, on a question which was at that time dividing the theologians, namely, whether the Incarnate Lord had one will or two. He replied to the Patriarch with a theological disquisition, in the course of which, after careful argument, he stated: 'We confess one will of our Lord Jesus Christ.' That is to say, he espoused the cause of the Monothelites, those who ascribed to Christ, after His Incarnation, one will only, and that one divine. His words on the subject, widely publicized, gave a strong fillip to the spread of Monothelite views. But in 649

Pope St Martin I and his Lateran Synod condemned Monothelitism as heretical. The dispute went on, however, and in 680 the Emperor summoned a Council, the sixth General Council, to meet at Constantinople. The Council, in pursuance of a letter sent by Pope Agatho, condemned Monothelitism, and proceeded to expel from the Church, among others, Pope Honorius, and to burn his letters on the subject as 'profane and soul-destroying'. Pope Leo II, soon after the Council, wrote to the Emperor: 'We anathematize . . . Honorius also, who did not illumine this apostolic see with the teaching of apostolic tradition, but by profane treachery allowed the spotless faith to be polluted.' The seventh General Council repeated the anathematization in 787, and until the eleventh century every Pope on the day of his election swore his acceptance of the decrees of the sixth General Council, which 'bound by eternal anathema the authors of the new heretical dogma . . . , together with Honorius, because he added fuel to their wicked assertions'.

It is, of course, the Roman Catholic case that Honorius's utterances were not made *ex cathedra* in the meaning given to it by the Vatican Council, and that therefore the doctrine of papal infallibility is not affected by his errors. Equally of course, the decree of the Vatican Council was framed with the notorious case of Honorius in mind, and therefore in such a way that his pronouncements could be held to fall outside its scope. The ground given for not counting them as uttered *ex cathedra* is that they were not issued to the universal Church, but only contained in a letter to the Patriarch of Jerusalem. But this, surely, is a lame defence, since Honorius plainly intended that his letter should be widely read and believed by all; and the doctrine of papal infallibility is in a precarious position if it hangs by such a slender thread as the virtual accident (or was it an act of Providence?) that a theological letter from the Pope was addressed to a Patriarch rather than to the Church at large. The embarrassment caused by Honorius's misdemeanours to the Roman apologists is shown by the fact that some of them hold that

Honorius intended to teach the whole Church *ex cathedra*, and that his statements are not really heretical, while others hold that they were not uttered *ex cathedra*, and were very heretical indeed.

The doctrine of the infallibility of the Pope, therefore, is untenable in logic and disproved by history. But we are bound to ask how such an error has captured the allegiance of hundreds of millions of men and women, many of them highly intelligent. The answer is not really far to seek. It springs, like the general doctrine of the infallibility of the Roman Church, of which it is only a specialized expression, from two sources: firstly, the desire, laudable enough, though misguided, to provide for the troubled and perplexed members of the human race an exact, unquestionable answer to the problems of life, and so to neutralize the consequences of human finitude; secondly, the not so laudable pride, the titanism, which creeps into the souls of men and groups of men who wield great influence over the lives of others, and tempts them to claim sacredness, immunity from criticism, and finally divinity, for their notions and purposes. And the Roman Church has imposed this doctrine upon men so successfully because in every age, and not least in our own, there are thousands of educated men and women who long desperately for the kind of security from doubt which Rome never ceases to offer. But the offer is a snare and a deceit: for God grants us faith, not certainty, and any attempt to circumvent this belies the human situation.

Whatever its source and origin, the doctrine of the infallibility of the Church, and of the Pope in particular, is the source and origin of nearly all the evil things which have disgraced the fair name of Rome. For when men belong to an institution to which they believe God to have given the gift of infallibility, they are immedia ly carried in their minds above the ordinary laws of right and truth. They cannot be wrong in action or in thought, and therefore any case that may be made out against them from outside their organization is false from the

beginning, and there is no room or need for argument.
Teaching which is contrary to their doctrine is not only
false, but also dangerous, because it is liable to seduce
the ignorant from the truth by which alone they can be
saved, and therefore to lead straight to their eternal
damnation. The enemies of the truths which they proclaim are the enemies of God Himself, and no ruthless-
ness is prohibited to those who seek to destroy the enemies
of God. To tolerate, to listen to the arguments of, those
who deny the doctrines of Rome is to play fast and loose
with the truth divinely revealed; to allow Protestants to
preach and teach in circumstances where they can be
prevented from doing so is to subvert the souls of men.

Thus we must ascribe, directly or indirectly, to the
doctrine of infallibility such things as the pitiless massacre
of Albigensians and Waldensians, the burning of John
Hus at the Council of Constance after he had been given
a safe conduct, the shameless exploitation of spiritual
power for personal and political ends by the later medieval Popes, the tortures and executions sanctioned by the
Holy Inquisition, the burning of Cranmer, Hooker,
Ridley, and Latimer, the fires of Smithfield, the vow of
the Jesuits to declare that black is white if the Church
so announces it, the education of children in such a way
that they never hear what is taught by Protestants, the
modern persecution of Protestants in Spain and other
countries where the Roman Catholic Church is supreme,
and the command frequently given by parish priests to a
woman to continue to conceive children when the doctor
has said that another childbirth will end her life.[1]

[1] In case it be thought that Rome has now abandoned her intolerance,
here are the words of Mgr R. A. Knox, written in 1927: 'You cannot
bind over the Catholic Church, as the price of your adhesion to her doctrine, to waive all right of invoking the secular arm in defence of her own
principles. The circumstances in which such a possibility could be realized
are sufficiently remote. . . . Given such circumstances, is it certain that
the Catholic Government of the nation would have no right to insist on
Catholic education being universal (which is a form of coercion) and even
to deport or imprison those who unsettle the minds of its subjects with
new doctrines? It is "certain" that the Church would claim the right for
the Catholic Government, even if considerations of prudence forbade its
exercise in fact.' He continues a little later: 'A body of Catholic patriots,

E

And if it be said that Protestants have ordered or countenanced many things like these, the answer must be that this, indeed, is most lamentably true; we do not wish to excuse or explain away the burning of Servetus by John Calvin or the tyrannies of the New England Puritans. But these and other evil things in the record of Protestantism also sprang from a doctrine of infallibility; and the falsity of all doctrines of infallibility has now been discovered and acknowledged by us, so that toleration, equal justice, and respect for the rights of individuals and minorities now flourish on Protestant soil wherever their fragile and delicate growth has not been mutilated by the advance of the totalitarian State. It may be that Protestants have repented of intolerance too late, but at least they have repented. The Roman Catholic Church has not, and, while it maintains its doctrine of infallibility, cannot!

entrusted with the government of a Catholic State, will not shrink from repressive measures in order to perpetuate the secure domination of Catholic principles among their fellow-countrymen' (*The Belief of Catholics*, p. 241) The Monsignor is at least frank.

CHAPTER TEN

The Cult of Mary

WE HAVE seen some of the ill effects of the doctrine of infallibility in the sphere of Christian ethics. In the sphere of Christian theology it has been equally disastrous. What has happened here is not so much that the doctrine has led directly to error, but that errors otherwise reached have been buttressed, perpetuated, and made articles of faith by means of it. The most conspicuous example of this is Mariology.

Protestants intend no disrespect of any kind to the mother of Jesus when they criticize the doctrines that have arisen about her or the religious devotion which is paid to her. They honour her most sincerely as the human agent, chosen because of her piety, humility, and faith, by whom the Saviour of the world was brought to birth, nourished, lovingly cared for, and given that education in the home which helped to prepare Him for His life's work. They profoundly sympathize with her sorrows and cares on His behalf, and with the agonizing grief occasioned by His death. They humbly admire her patient trust in the goodness of God and her acceptance of the place that was made for her in the affection of the early Church. They confess the doctrine of the Virgin Birth, and find great inspiration for Christian womanhood of every generation in her words at the Annunciation: 'Behold the handmaid of the Lord; be it unto me according to thy word.'

But we cannot hold her to be more than a woman endowed to a high degree with Christian qualities. We do not know, from any well-attested source of information, any more of her than that, and to suppose that she was any more than that runs clean contrary to all the impressions made on us by the very infrequent references to her in the New Testament. The structure of doctrine about her which has been erected on a completely post-biblical foundation fills us with alarm and distress. In no point do we regard the Roman Church as having gone farther astray from the Scriptural pattern of belief than in this.

The first doctrine about Mary to be enunciated beyond the Scriptural one of the Virgin Birth of Christ was that of her perpetual virginity. By the middle of the second century it was widely held in Christian circles that virginity was spiritually superior to the married state. This view relied on no support from the Gospels, where there is no trace of it at all (but rather the exaltation of the married state); but it could find confirmation in one side (though only one side) of Pauline teaching. Its real origin is probably not biblical at all, but is to be found in the need for a protest against the sexual immorality of paganism, and in non-Christian, Oriental, Gnostic ideas about the evil inherent in the human body. However this may be, the view gained wide currency, so wide, indeed, that Clement of Alexandria stands alone among the Christian Fathers in regarding matrimony as superior to celibacy. From this view the inference began to be drawn that Mary, as the mother of Jesus and certainly a virgin when she gave birth to Him, must have remained a virgin throughout her life. No Scriptural evidence was forthcoming for this; the whole argument for it is summed up in the words of Origen: 'Some persons, on the ground of the tradition contained in the Gospel according to Peter or the Book of James,[1] affirm that the brothers of Jesus were Joseph's sons by a former wife. Those who hold this view wish to preserve the honour of Mary in virginity to the end, in order that her body, once chosen for so high a purpose, might not be degraded to lower use after the Holy Spirit had come upon her; . . . and I think it reasonable that, as Jesus

[1] The reference is to two Apocryphal Gospels, which are not, of course, accepted as Scripture by either Protestants or Roman Catholics.

was the first-fruit of purity among men, so Mary should be among women.'[1]

Such *a priori* reasoning for the perpetual virginity of Mary can scarcely be regarded as strong in itself. And it is contradicted by the evidence of Scripture. Matthew says: 'And Joseph arose from his sleep, and did as the angel of the Lord commanded him, and took unto him his wife; and knew her not till she had brought forth a son' (Matthew 1[24]). The word 'knew' certainly refers to carnal knowledge, and the plain implication of the passage for everyone not committed to a particular doctrine is that after the birth of Jesus Joseph and Mary entered on the ordinary relationships of married life. Luke says: 'She brought forth her first-born son' (Luke 2[7]). Does not this verse just as plainly imply that Jesus was the first of several children?[2]

There are several references throughout the New Testament to the 'brothers' of Jesus and some to his 'sisters'. St Jerome held and popularized the theory that 'brothers' and 'sisters' here means 'cousins'. But there is a complete lack of linguistic evidence for this tortuous view, except for very rare cases where a writer makes it perfectly plain by the context that, although for some special reason he uses the word 'brother', he is actually referring to a cousin. This theory can therefore be disregarded. Only slightly more plausible is the 'Epiphanian' view, mentioned in the passage just quoted from Origen, that Jesus' brothers and sisters were children of

[1] *Commentary on Matthew* 10[17].

[2] Mgr R. A. Knox's footnote to his translation of Matthew 1[25] is instructive. In the text, following the Vulgate, he translates: 'and he had not known her when she bore a son, her first-born, to whom she gave the name Jesus'. In the footnote he acknowledges that the text would be more literally rendered by 'he knew her not till she bore a son', and comments: 'but the Hebrew word represented by "till" does not imply that the event which might have been expected *did* take place afterwards (cf. Genesis 8[7], Psalm 109[2], Daniel 6[24], 1 Maccabees 5[54])'. It is hardly necessary to point out that the original of the New Testament is in Greek, not Hebrew. But no Hebrew word meaning 'till' fails to imply what Knox says that it does not imply, and the linguistic evidence which he quotes is useless for his purpose. This is surely a clear case of maintaining an *a priori* thesis in the teeth of the chief evidence which we have.

Joseph by a former marriage. It is immediately clear that, since Jesus was not the son of Joseph, his 'brothers' and 'sisters', on this view, were not brothers and sisters at all, and we must suppose that those who refer to them as such were ignorant either of the Virgin Birth or of Joseph's earlier marriage and its issue. But two of the writers who do so refer to them are St Matthew and St Luke, on whom we rely for our knowledge of the Virgin Birth; and we must therefore conclude that St Matthew and St Luke at least did not know who Jesus' brothers and sisters were—which is surely very strange indeed. It may be added, as a supplementary point, that whenever the mother and brethren of Jesus appear in the Gospels they do so as a closely-knit family group, in a manner unlikely if the brethren of Jesus were not the children of His mother.

From all this the conclusion is hard to resist that belief in the perpetual virginity of Mary is the product of un-enlightened piety, that a historical event is asserted against the historical evidence, and that it has been accepted by millions of the faithful only because it is proclaimed by a Church which claims to be infallible. Without the false doctrine of infallibility it would hardly be accepted by any informed person.

This is not the place to recount how the cult of Mary has grown through the centuries, until now she occupies a place in the devotion of the Roman Catholic Church only a little lower than that given to the Persons of the Trinity, and is for many Roman Catholics nearer and more real than the Father, the Son, or the Holy Spirit. For this, we may pause to say, there are many causes, but chiefly two. The first is that Christian theology for many centuries during the Dark and Middle Ages made both the Father and the Son so remote and metaphysical in being, and sometimes so terrible in judgement, and the Holy Spirit so impersonal, that the simple believer turned to the warm, affectionate, protective qualities of the Virgin for the compassion and graciousness which seemed to him to be lacking in God. The second is that belief in a mother-goddess, taking many different forms, is a permanent part of the pre-Christian European and Near-Eastern religious tradition, and that the Virgin was all too easily identified with the local goddesses of a thousand different cities and countries, so that the immemorial rites of the Earth Mother could be transferred to her, with a purification of their grosser aspects, but often without a fundamental change.

We are here much more concerned, however, with the doctrines that have arisen out of the developing cult, the doctrines of the Immaculate Conception and the Bodily Assumption. Both of these have been only recently defined and made matters of faith for every Roman Catholic but they have been widely believed for many hundreds of years. The doctrine of the Immaculate Conception of the Blessed Virgin Mary, as defined by Pope Pius IX, speaking *ex cathedra* in 1854, 'holds the Blessed Virgin Mary to have been, from the first instant of her conception, by a singular grace and privilege of Almighty God, in view of the merits of Christ Jesus the Saviour of mankind, preserved free from all stain of original sin'.

The motive for ascribing such a privilege to the Mother of God is plain; the arguments are not convincing. Those from Scripture are virtually non-existent. The Vulgate of Genesis 3[15] reads 'she shall bruise thy [i.e. the serpent's] head', and it is urged that Mary could scarcely do this if she had any taint of Original Sin; but since the Vulgate has certainly mistranslated the Hebrew, which reads '*it* shall bruise thy head', and refers to the seed of Eve, we need not enter on any discussion of this. Theologically, weight is laid on the theory—a theory which appears as early as the writings of Tertullian—that as Christ, the second Adam, recapitulated the experiences of the first Adam, and at every point at which he was defeated by sin, defeated sin, so Mary, the second Eve, defeated the sins which defeated the first Eve. If this is true, it is argued, she could scarcely have needed to be redeemed herself, and therefore must have been free from Original Sin. This argument falls very far short of proof, and when we remember that Christ redeemed the whole of mankind, and that we are nowhere in Scripture given the slightest inkling that Mary was a sinless exception to the whole of mankind, we are bound to conclude that Mary, for all her goodness, needed to be saved, and was saved, by her Son.

Once again, surely, we have an example of a doctrine that would not be believed as a matter of necessary faith, though it might be held as a pious opinion, by informed Christians, unless it had been laid down and enforced by infallible authority. Once again error has received the imprimatur of infallibility.

Pope Pius XII announced *ex cathedra* in 1950 'that it is a dogma divinely revealed that the Immaculate Mother of God, Mary Ever Virgin, when the course of her life was finished, was taken up body and soul into heaven'. The Scriptural evidence for this is, by common consent, extremely slight. Revelation 12[1-6] gives a description of a 'woman arrayed with the sun', who bore a child which was 'caught up unto God, and unto his throne', while she herself fled into the wilderness, 'where she hath a place prepared by God'. This is taken by the Roman Catholic Church, as a description of the experiences of Mary, and thus the first verse of the chapter, which says of the woman that the moon was under her feet, and upon her head a crown of twelve stars, is interpreted as referring to her bodily assumption. But it will clearly bear very little weight as evidence for an alleged historical event of a miraculous and unique character. Nor is any historical evidence of any sort offered which is worthy of serious consideration—nothing more solid is provided than some apocryphal writings of the fourth century. The whole case admittedly rests on *tradition*, in the sense of a conscious belief in the Church today as proving the mind of the early Church, and is ratified by an infallible decree of the Pope. It is the ratification by the Pope that really establishes the doctrine; for there are many conscious beliefs in the Roman Catholic Church today which have not the status of necessary doctrine, and never will have that status unless the Pope infallibly declares in their favour. Yet again, we have a doctrine for which no argument with good theological credentials has been produced, but which is asserted by infallibility.

The effect of these three Mariological doctrines is to place the uniqueness and sole mediatorship of Christ in grave danger of denial. It is true that what is ascribed to Mary in orthodox Roman Catholic devotion is not worship (*latreia*) but high veneration (*hyperdoulia*, an intense form of the *doulia* which is paid to the saints). It is true that the faithful ask Mary to pray to her Son for them, and do not ask her to grant their prayers herself. But we are bidden in Scripture to make all our requests in the name of Jesus Christ, and Scripture knows of no need for an extra mediator. By current Roman Catholic practice in many lands the devotion actually paid to Mary goes far beyond official formularies, and official formularies during the last hundred years have shown every sign of keeping very close behind popular devotion. Every development in official doctrine about Mary leads to the painful conclusion that her status is becoming less and less human, and more nearly divine. It is not absurd to think that we may one day find her promoted to the position of a fourth Person in the Trinity as co-Redemptress with Christ; and then Christianity in its Roman Catholic form will have sunk into polytheism.

Thus the Roman Catholic Church, misled by sub-Christian piety, and confirmed in its errors by its doctrine of infallibility, has travelled a vast distance away from the faith of the Apostles, and the limit to its errors has not yet been set.

CHAPTER ELEVEN

Two Additional Errors

THE TWO further errors of Rome with which this book will be concerned are not of the same moment as those already dealt with, for they move largely within the sphere of pure dogmatics, and do not so directly touch the religious life of faithful Christian people. The doctrine of transubstantiation does not prevent a Roman Catholic from receiving the blessings of the Eucharist, and the inaccuracies of the Vulgate, especially as so finely translated into English by Mgr Ronald Knox, do not exclude him from reading and profiting by the Word of God in Scripture. But they are serious enough to deserve brief comment.

According to the Council of Trent (in Chapter 4 of the *Decree concerning the Most Holy Sacrament of the Eucharist*), 'by the consecration of the bread and wine, a conversion is made of the whole substance of the bread into the substance of the body of Christ our Lord, and of the whole substance of the wine into the substance of his blood; which conversion is, by the Holy Catholic Church, suitably and properly called Transubstantiation'. Now this doctrine is one of many possible interpretations of the words of Jesus, 'This is My body', 'This is my blood'. It has a genuinely religious basis; it seeks to theologize satisfactorily about a spiritual experience that has been shared ever since the beginning of the Christian Church by Christians of every communion. No argument that can be brought for or against it affects the reality of that experience, and it is a matter of common knowledge that Christians of very different theological approaches to the Eucharist have partaken of it together to the great benefit of their souls. Nor does a denial of its truth carry with it any kind of denial of the Real Presence of Christ among His servants at the Sacrament. The question at issue is simply the manner and mode of that Real Presence.

Scripture does not offer a theological interpretation of the Eucharist. But the doctrine of transubstantiation does not very easily cohere with what it has to say about its celebration and religious significance. There is a certain absurdity in the suggestion that Christ meant that the bread and wine at the Last Supper had been converted into the substance of His body and blood when He was present Himself in the flesh, in body and blood, at the Supper. Nor is it in accord with the general tenor of New Testament teaching about the Risen Christ that His body and blood should be from time to time localized in material things. But on these points, no doubt, a legitimate difference of opinion could persist. The fundamental objection to the doctrine of Transubstantiation is that it weds Christian theology to a particular philosophical theory, which was never more than one among many possible explanations of the universe of experience, and has now probably been finally exploded.

For, to uphold the theory, we must believe that material objects possess both substance and accidents, substance being an invisible, intangible, imperceptible something in virtue of which the thing is what it is and nothing else, and the accidents being those properties of the thing which can be apprehended by the senses—its colour, shape, size, and so on. If we are willing to agree thus far, we can go on to say that at the moment of the consecration of the elements in the Eucharist, the substance of the bread and wine is converted into the substance of the body and blood of Christ, while the accidents remain as they were before. No one can deny that this is a subtle and ingenious theory, nor claim that such a conversion is beyond God's power. The difficulty is that it is very hard nowadays to believe in the doctrine of substance and accidents at all, in respect of any part of the material universe. Without going into philosophical technicalities, we can safely say that after severe criticism by John Locke, the doctrine was abandoned by Berkeley, Hume, and all subsequent philosophers, except by those within the Roman Catholic Church (who have a vested interest in it), and now it is hardly ever mentioned in philosophical discussions. The doctrine might, of course, come back into philosophical currency, but never as more than one possible theory among many, and it was surely unwise and temerarious of the Roman Church at the Council of Trent to bind it on the faithful when the evidence for it was not, and never can be, conclusive. It came from the teaching of the Schoolmen, basing themselves upon Aristotle, and in the sixteenth century it was not considered possible by Roman Catholic theologians that the main Scholastic doctrines could ever be called in question. But some of them have been called in question, and this particular one has been shown to be virtually impossible.

We turn to another indiscretion of the Council of Trent. After giving a definitive list of the books of Sacred Scripture which includes the Old Testament Apocrypha, it lays down that the 'old and vulgate edition, which by the lengthened usage of so many ages, has been approved of in the Church, be, in public lectures, disputations, sermons, and expositions, held as authentic; and that no one is to dare or presume to reject it under any pretext whatever' (*Decree concerning the Edition and the Use of the Sacred Books*). St Jerome's translation of the Scriptures, known as the Vulgate, is here defined as the authentic text of the Bible, and every Roman Catholic is required to believe that it is so. St Jerome used for his translation the best texts of the Hebrew Old Testament, the Greek Apocrypha and the Greek New Testament available in his time, and translated with considerable skill and exactness. But no one could seriously deny that he has made a number of mistakes in translation, as our modern knowledge plainly demonstrates (that is, if human reason can be said to demonstrate anything—and it is Roman Catholic doctrine that it can demonstrate a great deal). Moreover, manuscripts of both the Old and New

Testaments have been discovered since his time—several of them before the meeting of the Council of Trent—which are undoubtedly nearer to the original writings than any which St Jerome had at his disposal. In any case, the Vulgate is a translation, not the original text; and no translation is, or can be, authentic in the sense in which the original text is authentic. Thus the Decree of the Council, passed in a pre-critical age, is demonstrably false to the facts, and can be nothing but an embarrassment to honest Roman Catholic scholars, as can be clearly seen by the shifts to which Mgr Knox is reduced when he seeks both to translate the Vulgate and to give the sense of the original at the same time.

The cloak of infallibility can be thrown over these problems, but it does not succeed in concealing or solving them.

The Hope of Reunion

THE Roman Catholic Church genuinely and per-
sistently desires the reunion of all Christian people.
It has announced the terms on which the Churches not
in communion with it can be restored to communion
with it; and the terms amount to complete submission
to the claims of the Roman Pontiff.

It is inconceivable that the Orthodox or Protestant
Churches will ever accept such terms. There is, and will
be, no wavering in their conviction that Rome has
grievously divagated from orthodoxy in many points, and
that, in particular, the supremacy of the Pope is completely unacceptable.

The Roman Catholic Church has more and more
firmly since the Reformation placed itself in a position
from which there can be no retreat, by not only declaring
the doctrines which Protestants hold to be false but also
declaring itself infallible in the declaration of them. It
has made it impossible for it ever to admit that it has
been mistaken without destroying itself for ever.

Is there, then, no hope of reunion? The human eye
can see no hope whatever. Yet Roman Catholic and
Protestant theologians are conversing about matters of
doctrine in France and Germany; Roman Catholic ob-
servers are present at the Assemblies of the World Council
of Churches; in Great Britain and elsewhere, under certain conditions, Roman Catholic and Protestant speakers
may give addresses about reunion on the same platform
during the Octave of Prayer for Christian Unity. May
we not pray that Rome may become willing to enter
fully into the ecumenical conversation, where the
Churches do not seek to convert each other, but only

to mould the beliefs of all into the glorious wholeness of Christian truth? And if she were to become willing, can it not be that the Holy Spirit will even now guide us forward into 'the unity of the Spirit in the bond of peace'?